THE MANDOLIN PICKER'S FAKEBOOK

THE MANDOLIN PICKER'S FAKEBOOK

By David Brody

Oak Publications
New York•London•Sydney

Cover design and illustration by Mona Conner
Book design by Diane Stevens
Edited by Patricia Ann Neely and Peter Pickow

© 1993 Oak Publications
A Division of Embassy Music Corporation, New York
All Rights Reserved

Order Number: OK 64352
International Standard Book Number: 0.8256.0239.4

Exclusive Distributors:
Music Sales Corporation
257 Park Avenue South, New York, NY 10010 USA
Music Sales Limited
8/9 Frith Street, London W1V 5TZ England
Music Sales Pty. Limited
120 Rothschild Street, Rosebery, Sydney, NSW 2018, Australia

Printed in the United States of America by
Vicks Lithograph and Printing Corporation

FOREWORD

This book was undertaken to provide a companion folio to the *Fiddler's Fakebook*. As such it contains many of the tunes from the latter arranged specifically for the mandolin and transcribed in tablature. In the preparation of this volume I have remained close to the text of the *Fiddler's Fakebook* making only such changes as were necessitated by differences between the two instruments.

The collection has been drawn from many musical traditions from both the British Isles and North America. At least several of these traditions have no ancient or pronounced history of mandolin playing. The modern tendency seems to be to adapt to the mandolin what was the melodic, tune-playing role of the harp and pipe, and in later musics that of the fiddle (which on both sides of the Atlantic became the dominant dance-tune instrument*).

The tunes that follow were chosen because of their general popularity, their adaptability to the mandolin, and with a view of covering a wide range of styles.

*One must also acknowledge the melodic role of the banjo. Among blue-grass players, fiddle tunes are commanded in 'Keith style'. Among the frailers, note-for-note renderings are accomplished in the 'melodic clawhammer style'. In recent decades the guitar has also taken on the melodic challenge and in the hands of such virtuosi as Clarence White, Doc Watson, Dan Crary, and Tony Rice it has bounded into the arena of the fiddle tune.

CONTENTS

The Tunes

PREFACE

This book was conceived two years ago, almost to the day, at a time when I was teaching fiddle and mandolin in New York City. It was my idea then, with my students in mind, to compile a book of the most often played, most important and most interesting fiddle tunes from the various Celtic and North American traditions.

The tunes were chosen by cataloguing a large number of recordings by tune title. A tally was taken to find out which had been recorded most often. This established a foundation of material that could not be left out. To this list I added the names of other pieces which had not been recorded as frequently, but which I knew were played regularly and with respect. I admit to sprinkling the collection with a few lesser known tunes which happen to be personal favorites, but I am sure they will hold their own when placed next to the old war horses of the repertoire.

The individual settings were developed after listening to a number of recordings of the same tune and then selecting one or two upon which to rely for the printed version. You can find this information in the General Discography.

In most cases I have indicated ornaments remembering how mysterious these seemed to me as I struggled during those first few years of playing to hear with an undeveloped and naive ear the rolls, triplets, trills, and slurs.

These nearly always eluded me as I hopelessly wore holes in my records, playing the same measure over and over. Consistent with this I have tried to keep settings uncluttered and distinct so that the rhythm and melody are easily read and do not have to be disentangled from a web of hieroglyphics.

The tunes which follow are not to be taken as the "right" or the "real" version. An application of these terms to a musical genre so wonderfully capable of change and variation as the fiddle tune, that chameleon in binary form, is to misconstrue its nature. This caution made, I believe that the settings in this volume do follow what is commonly agreed upon through usage as *the* melody and *the* rhythm for a particular piece.

In some sense all aural music is improvisational. You only begin to internalize the possibilities of variation and improvisation in a given style through repeated listening. Whether you are a complete beginner, or an advanced or classically trained musician, spend time listening. (See the Select Discography in the back of the book.) Listening to the real thing will give you more information than the most exact transcription. Reading music, especially when the essence of that music is aural, without a clear idea of how it should sound is like reading a foreign language of which you know the characters and are yet unfamiliar with their exact pronunciation and meaning.

In the preparation of the General Discography, several people were of help. Bob Carlin, Mick Moloney, Henry Sapoznik, Jerry Jenkins, and Alistair J. Hardie all gave me valuable title and discographical information.

The following record companies were generous in supplying many of the albums which made the General Discography possible:

Adelphi Records, American Heritage Records, Arhoolie Records, Biograph Records, Breakwater Records, Briar Records, The Country Dance and Song Society, CMH Records, County Records, Folkways Records, Fretless Records, Front Hall Records, Gael-Linn Records, GMI Records, Green Linnet Records, Green Mountain Records, June Appal Records, Kicking Mule Records, MAG Records, Mulligan Records, Omac Records, Outlet Records, Philo Records, Rebel Records, Ridge Runner Records, Rounder Records, Shanachie Records, Sonet Records, United Artists Records, Vetco Records, and Voyager Records.

Thanks also to my editors Pat Neely, Peter Pickow, and Jason Shulman.

INTRODUCTORY MATERIALS

Tune Titles

Different tunes often have a common name and certain tunes have more than one name. This unequal distribution of nominal wealth can lead to confusion. In an attempt to anticipate problems generated by what in some cases is a dearth and in other cases a cornucopia of titles I have cross-referenced and listed alternative titles in the Index. I have also coded certain of the tunes with Roman numerals, capital letters, and Arabic numerals as follows.

Roman numerals are used to distinguish unrelated tunes which have the same name. Titles which do not share the use of an article, but which are in all other ways alike, are also distinguished by the addition of a Roman numeral. Consequently, "The Bunch of Keys" and "Bunch of Keys" are marked respectively I and II.

Capital letters distinguish related tunes of the same name. Compare the A and B parts of "Money Musk A" with the C and A parts of "Money Musk B". It is clear that there is common melodic material but the differences make it impossible to consider one piece a variant of the other.

Arabic numerals mark diverse settings of the same tune. These settings are characterized by differences in style and approach.

This system of numbers and letters does not pretend to surgical precision. Things which have evolved in raucous chaos are susceptible to so much order before their nature, which one has only set out to clarify, is changed. Could they, the sprawling oceans would laugh at the cartographer who strives to confine their amorphous shape to unyielding paper. I have labeled these tunes optimistic of the simple practicality of doing so.

Tune titles correspond to those used in the *Fiddler's Fakebook*. Although there is only one version of "Arkansas Traveler" in the present volume there are three in the *Fiddler's Fakebook*. They are titled respectively; "Arkansas Traveler 1," "Arkansas Traveler 2," and "Arkansas Traveler 3." Since the version in this book corresponds to the second version in the *Fiddler's Fakebook* it bears the same title, "Arkansas Traveler 2." This will facilitate the matching of various settings when the two books are used conjointly.

Types of Tunes

Air

An air is a songlike melody which is usually played slowly. In contrast to the reel, hornpipe, and jig it is not a dance tune. It can be in duple ($\frac{2}{4}$), triple ($\frac{3}{4}$), or quadruple ($\frac{4}{4}$) meter. Certain of these tunes are played with a high degree of rubato.

Breakdown

This term is used rather loosely to refer to a wide range of up-tempo Old-Time and Bluegrass tunes in duple ($\frac{2}{4}$) and quadruple ($\frac{4}{4}$) meter.

Country Rag

In duple ($\frac{2}{4}$) or quadruple ($\frac{4}{4}$) meter, these tunes are usually in at least three and sometimes as many as five parts. They are invariably in the keys of F, C, G, and D and often modulate to the dominant or sub-dominant in the third part. They show a preference for the cadence chord progressions II V; I VI II V; and IV IV#°I VI II V. The country rag is always played in swing eighth notes:

(See also Rag)

Double Jig—Point Dúbalta

A jig in $\frac{6}{8}$ in which each eighth note is voiced.

(See also Jig)

Hoedown

A term synonomous with, but used less frequently than, breakdown. (See Breakdown)

Hornpipe—Cornphíopaí

Originally the name of an English dance dating from the Middle Ages, the hornpipe is in duple ($\frac{2}{4}$) or quadruple ($\frac{4}{4}$) meter. It is played more slowly than the reel and in a slightly altered rhythm which is expressed as follows:

Many tunes given the name 'hornpipe' are played as reels (e.g. "Rickett's Hornpipe"). The Scottish and Cape Breton fiddlers make a clear distinction between these two forms although many musicians will treat these identically.

Jig—Poirt

Any of the tunes in $\frac{6}{8}$ or $\frac{9}{8}$ used for the dance of the same name. This is primarily an Irish form. (See also Single Jig, Double Jig, Slip Jig, and the section Rhythm).

March

These tunes in $\frac{2}{4}$ and $\frac{6}{8}$ developed with the usage of music as accompaniment to processionals. The most common types are military and wedding marches.

Novelty Rag

The composed rag of tin-pan alley traced on the form of the classical rag. These tunes often fall into cliche patterns of melody and syncopation. Many were written, as the name indicates, to be novel. This often meant little more than giving the piece a silly or slapstick title or introducing it as a piece for an unusual instrument. (See also Rag)

Polka

A sprightly dance in duple meter ($\frac{2}{4}$) originating in Eastern Europe in the early nineteenth century. The paradigmatic rhythm is:

Quadrille

Originally the name of a nineteenth century French dance. Among fiddlers, tunes with this appellation are either in $\frac{2}{4}$ or $\frac{6}{8}$, more often the latter.

Quickstep

The tunes that I am aware of with this name are in duple ($\frac{2}{4}$) or quadruple ($\frac{4}{4}$) meter and are played much like reels. *The Harvard Dictionary of Music* reports that this was originally a military march, done, as the name would have it, in "quick steps." They go on to cite the number: 108 per minute.

Rag

A type of instrumental piece having at least three and as many as five parts each one of which is made up of sixteen or thirty-two measures. Its great epoch, that of classical ragtime, extended from the late nineteenth century into the first two decades of the twentieth. The outstanding quality of the rag is its use of certain simple patterns of syncopation like the following:

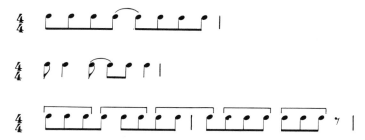

(See also Country Rag and Novelty Rag)

Reel—Ríleanna

The reel, in duple ($\frac{2}{4}$) and quadruple ($\frac{4}{4}$) meter is played in a wide variety of styles throughout the British Isles and North America. It is in binary form and the prevailing rhythm is:

Set Dance

An Irish tune associated with a specific dance is called a set dance. It can be in duple ($\frac{2}{4}$), triple ($\frac{3}{4}$), or quadruple ($\frac{4}{4}$) meter.

Single Jig—Poirt Singil

A jig in $\frac{6}{8}$ in which each eighth note is *not* voiced. The essential rhythmic pattern is:

(See also Jig)

Slide

A type of dance and tune found mainly in the southwest counties of Ireland. It is closely related to the jigs in $\frac{6}{8}$.

Slip Jig—Poirt Luascaigh

A variety of jig in $\frac{9}{8}$. The basic rhythmic pattern of the slip jig is:

Strathspey

Originating in northeastern Scotland the strathspey is a close relative of the hornpipe and reel. It is played at a slower tempo than either of the aforementioned and depends for its character on dotted rhythms like the following:

Waltz

A tune in $\frac{3}{4}$ meter used to accompany the dance of the same name. These tunes are not much played in the British Isles, but are a staple in the repertoire of the North American contest fiddler.

Composers

The great majority of the tunes in this volume, and of fiddle tunes in general, are without known authors. Some pieces are older than the modern instruments upon which we play them.*

Because most of this music was not written down, having been transmitted aurally, the names of the composers have been all but lost. When I have had information as to authorship I have included it in the heading above the tune. When certain sources claim that a fellow wrote a tune and others hold that he did not I have included the name but followed it with a question mark.

Genre

England

"The recorded fiddlers in England are few, which leads one to think that there never were many and that perhaps there never was a need for many." So writes John Timpany in his book on English fiddle playing.** ·

Since the early Middle Ages the church actively did its best to rid the island of the secular music and dance which had at its core pagan myth and ritual (e.g., Morris dancing). What has survived is a very simple style of tune playing and a handful of tunes (as compared with the riches of Ireland, Scotland, and Shetland). Ornament is used sparingly.

Scotland

The reels among the Scottish are played somewhat slower than in Ireland, and the roll, the staple Irish ornament is rarely heard. While in most traditional fiddling virtuosity resides in the left hand, in Scottish fiddling the right hand comes into its pyrotechnical own with a wide variety of arpeggio and spiccato bowings.

Ireland

The tunes abound on this small island where there are as many internal styles as counties. Generally speaking the attention paid to ornament is almost as great as that paid to the rhythm and melody.

Tunes in the Aeolian, Dorian, and Mixolydian modes are as common as those in the Ionian (major) mode.

Shetland

The tunes of Shetland are some of the most wonderful and yet in this country, under-played. I have done what I could to correct this by including a good number in the present collection. Owing something to Scotland and Ireland and something to Norway and Sweden, Shetland has a lively style all its own.

French Canadian

The French Canadian fiddlers have a good deal in common with their New England neighbors. There is a lot of borrowing from the Scottish and Irish repertoire, but, these tunes are often played in a less ornamented and more rhythmic style. The favored instrumentation is fiddle and piano.

Nova Scotia/Cape Breton

A style sharing many tunes and techniques with Scottish fiddling.

---

*The violin, mandolin, guitar, and banjo are comparative newcomers to Western dance music. Certainly in Ireland the pipes and harp were the dominant melody instruments before the inception of the fiddle in the mid-eighteenth century.

**Timpany, John. *"And out of his knapsack he drew a fine fiddle"* (London: The English Folk Dance and Song Society, 1973) p. 33.

New England

Many New England musicians hold danceability as the yardstick with which to measure a fiddler's playing. Some play in an ornamented style à la Irish or Scottish and some in a simpler English fashion. While many of the tunes are specifically New English (New English?) many are also of Celtic origin.

Old-Time

I have used this term to refer to the traditional fiddle music of the American South and Midwest; most notably that of Kentucky, Virginia, Arkansas, Tennessee, North Carolina, Mississippi, Alabama, Georgia, and South Carolina.

Bluegrass

Bluegrass grew out of Old-Time and Country music. It is a performance rather than a dance music and was invented and promulgated by Bill Monroe. A mandolinist himself, Monroe elevated his instrument to an executive position in the string hierarchy giving it a new and challenging rhythmic and melodic role.

Texas Style

Texas Style is played throughout the Western United States. The tunes are taken at a slower tempo than in either Old-Time or Bluegrass and the focus is on "hot" melodic improvisation.

Western Swing

Western Swing is a form of country music which was influenced by popular Swing. The fiddling often aspires to "hot" improvisation modeled on the playing of jazz soloists, notably violinist Joe Venuti.

Modes and Key Signatures*

The key indication for each piece is based on its modal scale rather than on a presumed major or minor scale. I have done this because it gives you, at a glance, a clear sense of the melodic and harmonic foundation of the piece.

Fiddle tunes in their modal make-up rarely go beyond two flats or three sharps, and those in one and two sharps seem to be the most common. The favored tonics are G, D, and A. C, F, and E follow, probably in that order, and B♭ and E♭ trail behind. The popular modes are Ionian (or Major), Mixolydian, Dorian, and Aeolian (or Natural Minor). Below I have put this into graphic terms showing the favored fiddle-tune key signatures and their related modes. Those in parentheses are not much used.

Ionian (Major)	B♭	F	C	G	D	A
Dorian	(F)	(C)	G	D	A	E
Mixolydian	(C)	G	D	A	E	(B)
Aeolian (Natural minor)	G	D	A	E	B	(F♯)

I have indicated the tonic and mode above the time signature as follows:

D Mixolydian

There are many tunes which show a lack of commitment to a single mode. Although faithful to a single tonic they will flirt with other scales. In such cases I have transcribed the piece in its most assertive mode.

In the headings where 'Ionian' was called for I have substituted 'Major'.

---

*If you are unfamiliar with modes, scales, key signatures, and the like you might find it helpful to research them in a dictionary or encyclopedia of music.

Tempo

The choice of how fast or slow a piece should be played is one that rests with the individual. The same musician may play a tune at widely different tempos depending on whether he is playing in concert, for dancers, or in his living room with friends. This is to say nothing of the differences in speed heard for a given tune among a number of musicians. If you attend a New England fiddle contest you are almost sure to hear at least a dozen versions of "Devil's Dream" ranging from a stately moderato to the vernacular *breakneck*. In addition you have diverse tempos for the same piece depending on the style in which it is played: Irish, New England, and Bluegrass musicians are each going to take "Temperance Reel" at a different speed.

General tempo is prescribed by reason and the exact choice is a function of taste. In preference to giving metronome settings I suggest listening.

Rhythm

Swing Eighth Notes

Many mandolinists do not take the mathematical reality of the eighth note seriously. This is especially true of Bluegrass, Texas, and Western Swing musicians and for the playing of rags. The tendency is to play eighth notes in what can be approximated as the following rhythm.

Jigs

Jigs are often played in dotted rhythms as follows:

Shuffle Rhythm

In many of the Old-Time and Bluegrass tunes notes of longer duration () can be played in a shuffle rhythm:

Here is a simplified version of the first two measures of "Arkansas Traveler":

Here it is again but with the addition of the shuffle:

Reading Tablature

Pitch is located through string and fret indications. Each space or track represents one of the mandolin's sets of double strings.

The open string is represented by placing a zero on a given track.

Open G

A number written on a given track indicates at what fret the string should be depressed. If I wanted you to play second fret on the G string (A), I would write it like this:

(A)

This could be held for any rhythmic value:

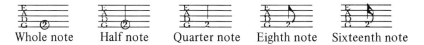

Whole note   Half note   Quarter note   Eighth note   Sixteenth note

To acquaint yourself with this system try reading this G major scale.

Symbols and Ornaments

Grace Notes

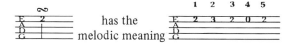

The notes which appear in small print are called *grace notes*. They are ordinarily considered a rhythmic part of the note to which they are connected by a phrasing mark. In the case where there is no phrasing mark they form a rhythmic part of the note which they precede.

The Roll or Turn

∾

This is the staple ornament of Irish fiddle. It consists of five notes as follows:

1. The prime note
2. The pitch a half or whole step higher than the prime note.
3. The prime note
4. The pitch a half or whole step lower than the prime note.
5. The prime note

has the melodic meaning

This configuration is played in a wide variety of rhythms:

is played   or

Certain brave fellows play a six-note roll which I have written like this:

If the fourth note of a roll is only a half step lower than the prime note it is not uncommon to slide down to it from the prime note and then slide back up.

The Four-Note Roll

I have used this symbol to represent those rolls of four notes which resolve on the next written note.

Slides

I have notated slides in the following ways:

SL Slide up into the note indicated from a pitch slightly below.

ʃLʃ Slide down into the note indicated from a pitch slightly above.

 Slide with the indicated finger from the first pitch to the second.

Octaves

Also 8va↑   Also 8va↓

I have used these symbols to indicate that a part, in addition to being played as written, may be played either an octave higher or lower.

Triplets

Triplets are often played ♩. ♪ ♩ and ♩. ♪ ♪ especially when they are used ornamentally in Celtic tunes.

As an upbeat to an Old-Time tune a triplet is often played like a series of grace notes.

Notes in Parentheses

(♩) These notes can be, but are not necessarily fully voiced.

Other Symbols

Accent >

Tremolo ≋ ≢

Trill *tr*

These symbols direct you to an explanation above the tune.

*

'* *

†

Drones

The droning of open strings to the accompaniment of the melody line is common in many styles of tune playing.

Here is the beginning of "La Bastringue" showing drone possibilities:

This can be applied to many of the tunes in this book.

THE TUNES

AFTER THE BATTLE OF AUGHRIM

Irish

ANGELINE THE BAKER 1

Old-Time

25

ANGUS CAMPBELL

Reel　　　　Scottish

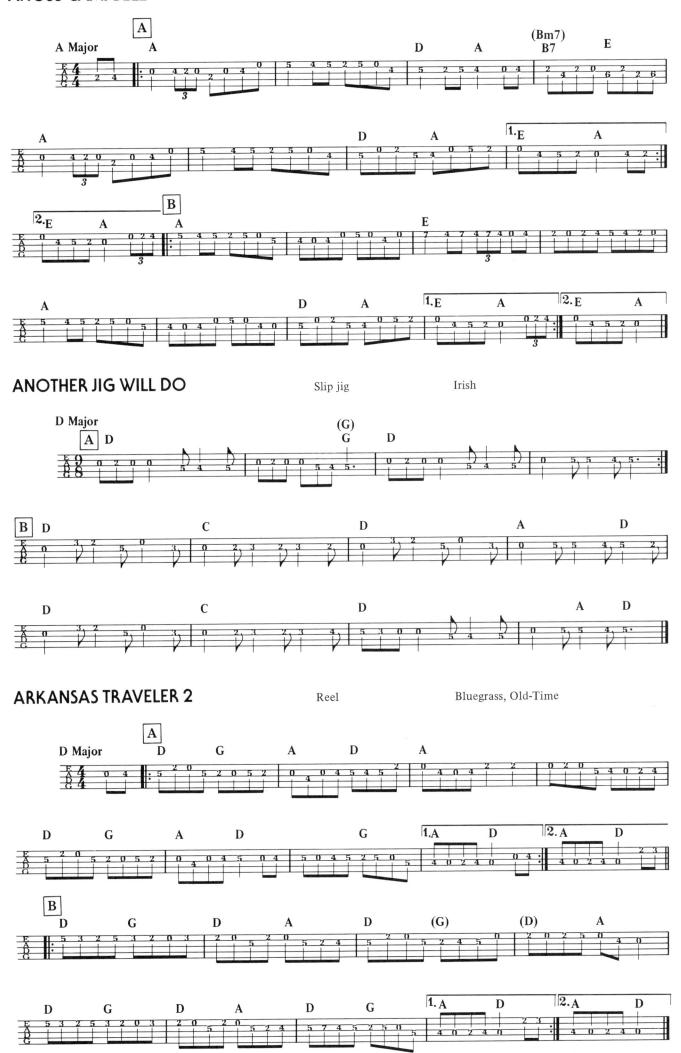

ANOTHER JIG WILL DO

Slip jig　　　　Irish

ARKANSAS TRAVELER 2

Reel　　　　Bluegrass, Old-Time

THE ATHOLL HIGHLANDERS

March   Scottish

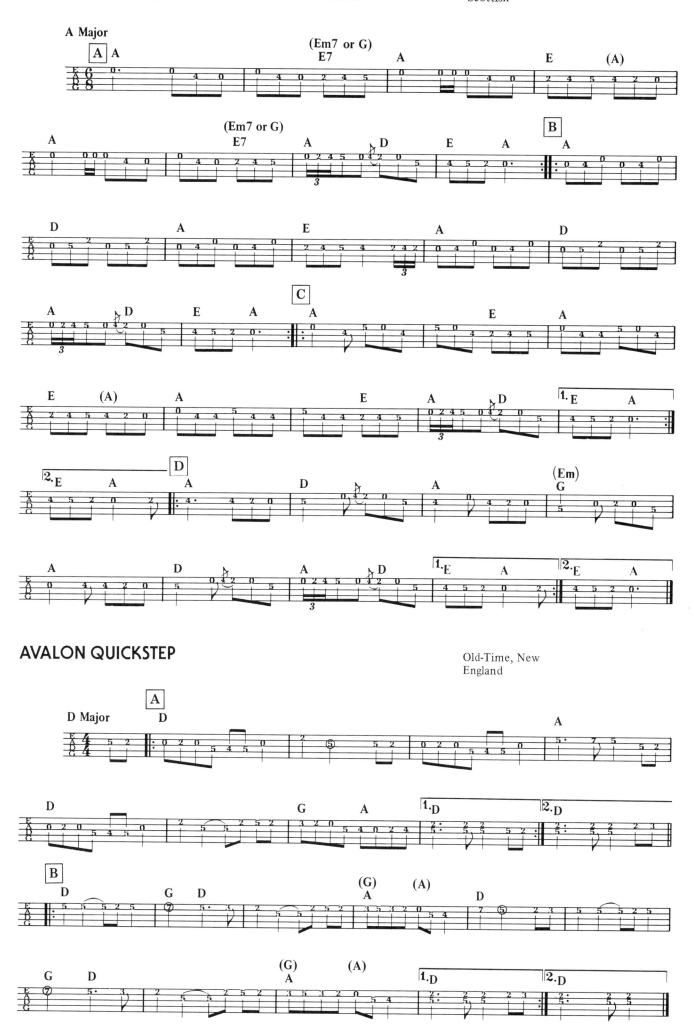

AVALON QUICKSTEP

Old-Time, New
England

BANISH MISFORTUNE

Double jig   Irish

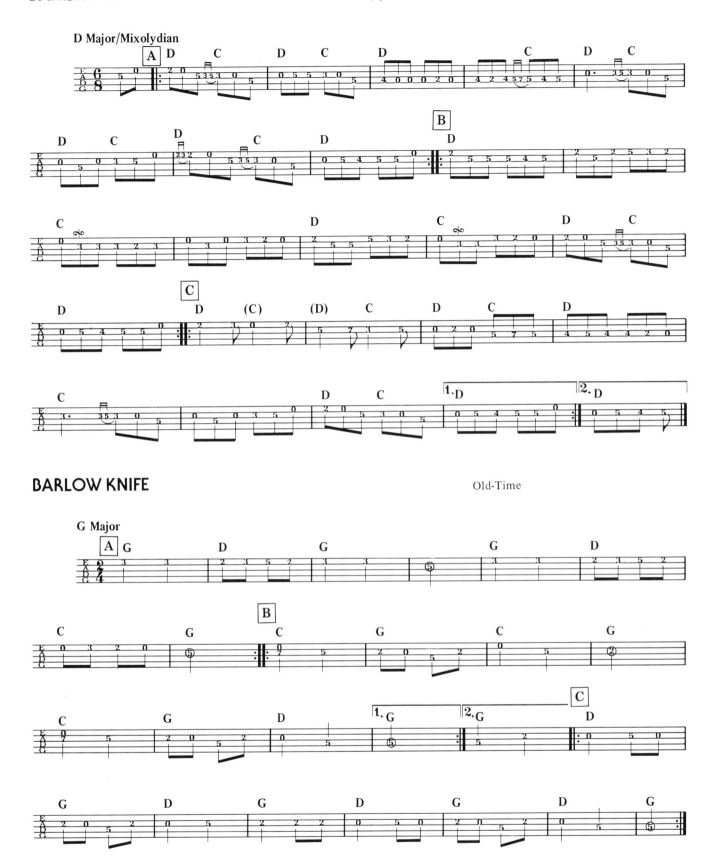

BARLOW KNIFE

Old-Time

LA BASTRINGUE

Reel   French Canadian

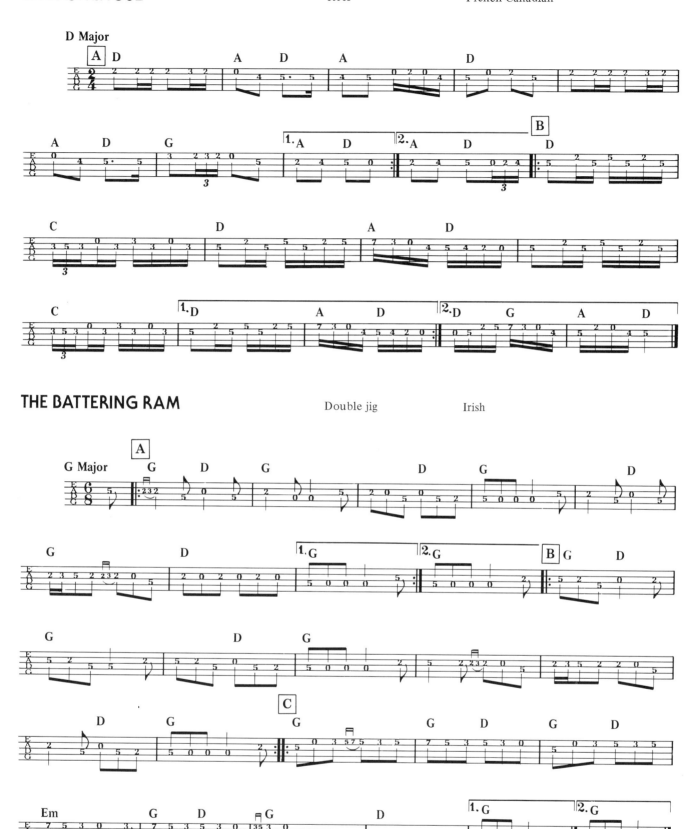

THE BATTERING RAM

Double jig   Irish

THE BATTLE OF AUGHRIM

Irish

BEAUMONT RAG

Bluegrass, Texas
Style, Western Swing

BIG SANDY RIVER

by Kenny Baker and   Bluegrass
Bill Monroe

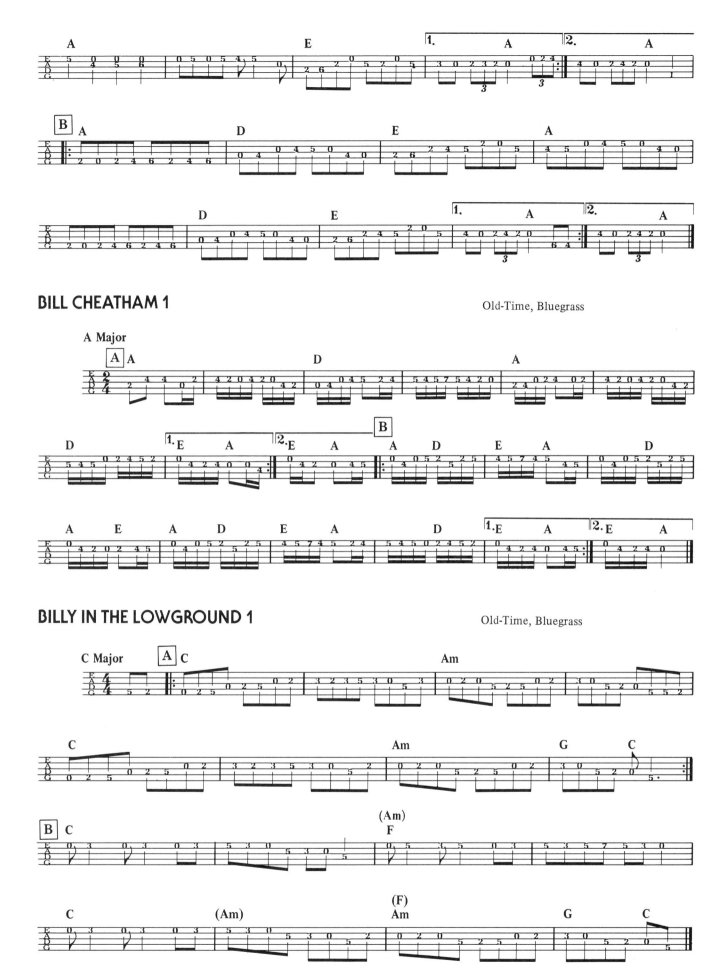

BILL CHEATHAM 1

Old-Time, Bluegrass

BILLY IN THE LOWGROUND 1

Old-Time, Bluegrass

BLACK AND WHITE RAG

Texas Style, Western
Swing

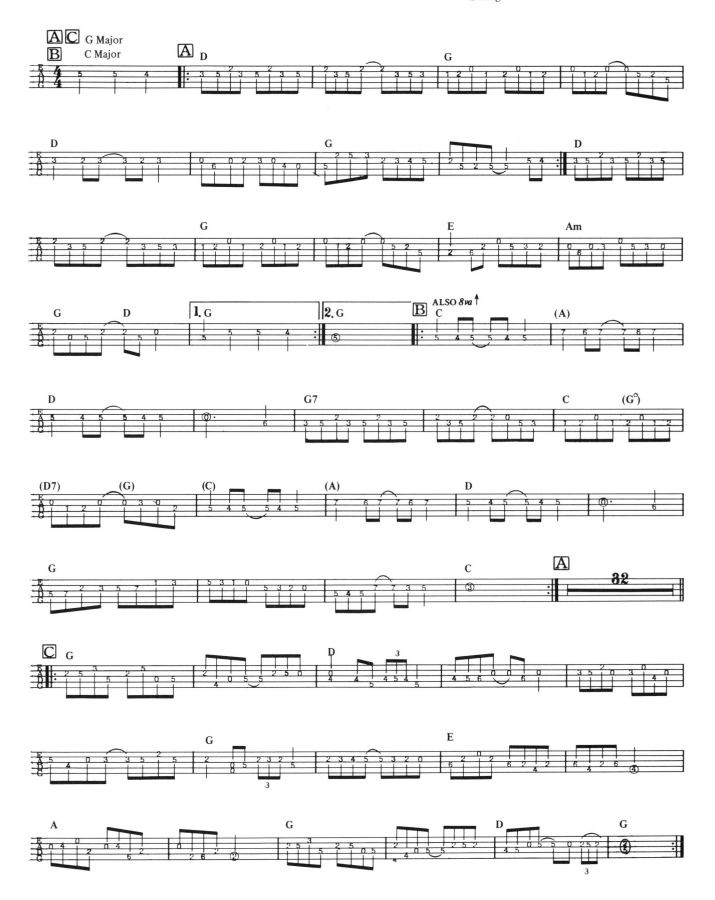

BLACKBERRY BLOSSOM I

Old-Time, Bluegrass

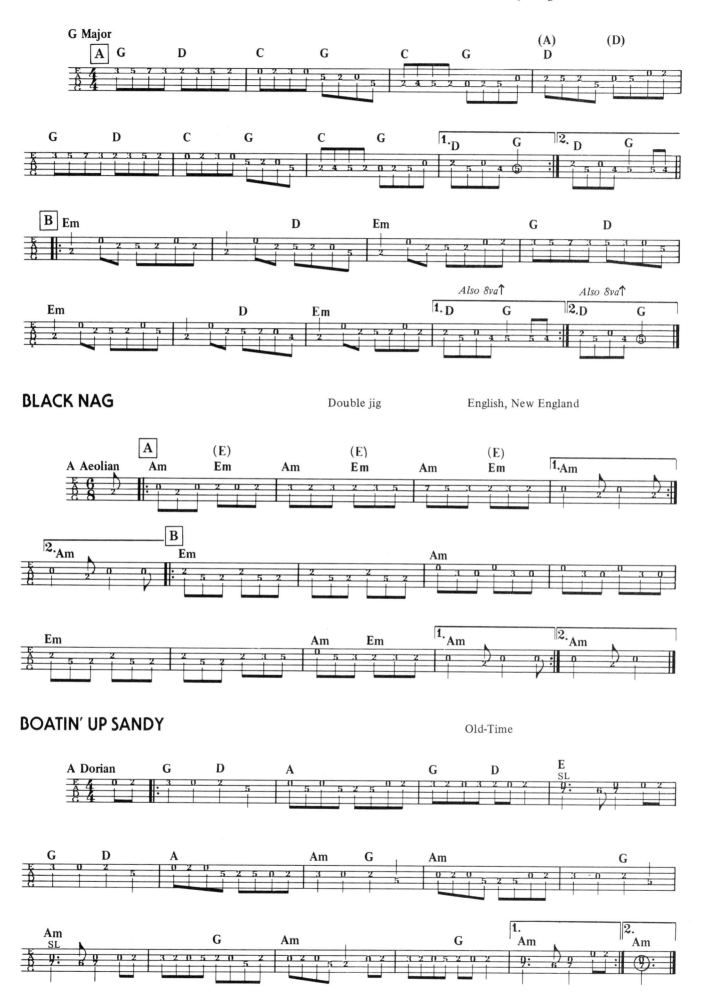

BLACK NAG

Double jig   English, New England

BOATIN' UP SANDY

Old-Time

BONAPARTE CROSSING THE RHINE

Old-Time

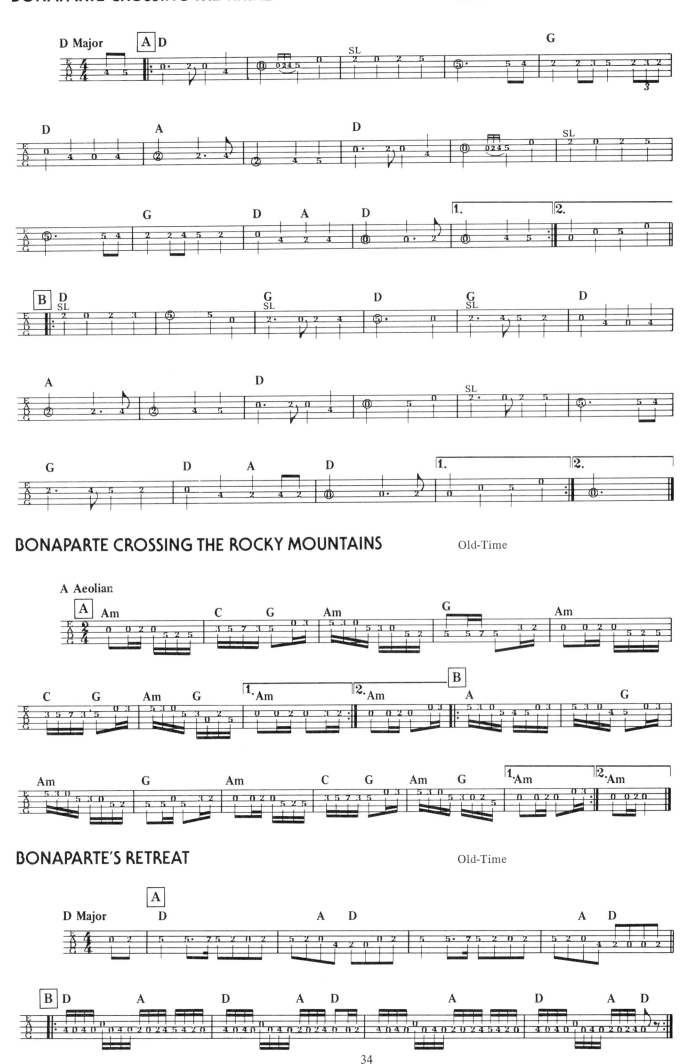

BONAPARTE CROSSING THE ROCKY MOUNTAINS

Old-Time

BONAPARTE'S RETREAT

Old-Time

BONNIE ISLE O' WHALSAY

Reel   Shetland

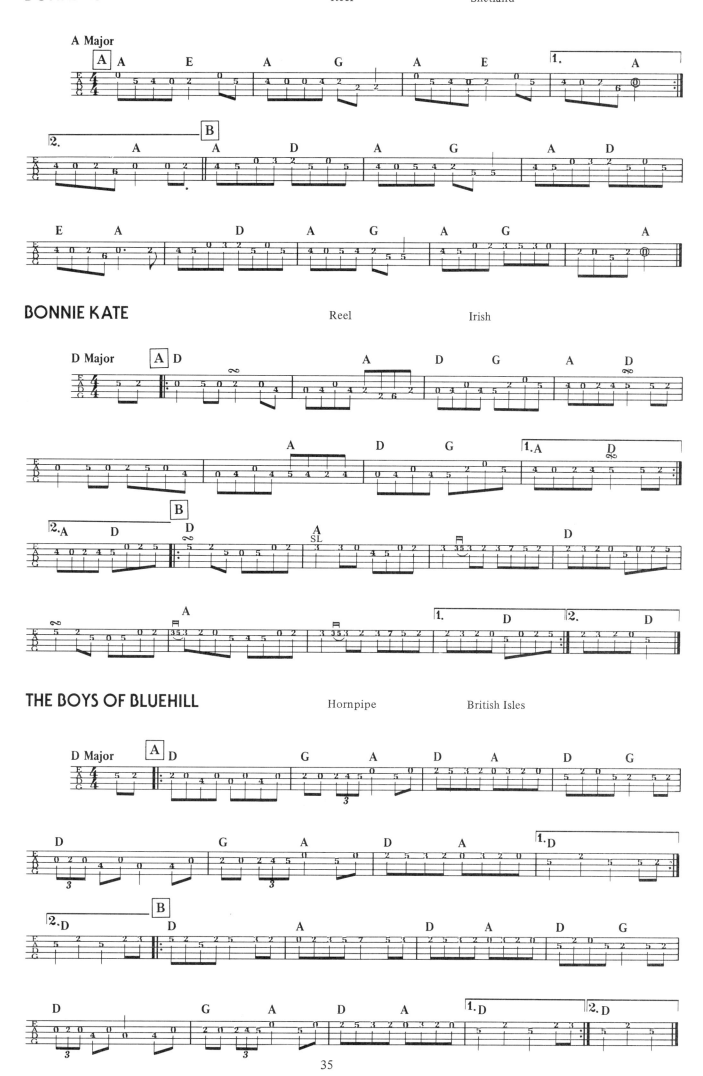

BONNIE KATE

Reel   Irish

THE BOYS OF BLUEHILL

Hornpipe   British Isles

BRIARPICKER BROWN

Old-Time

THE BRIDE'S A BONNIE THING

March   Shetland

BULL AT THE WAGON

Old-Time

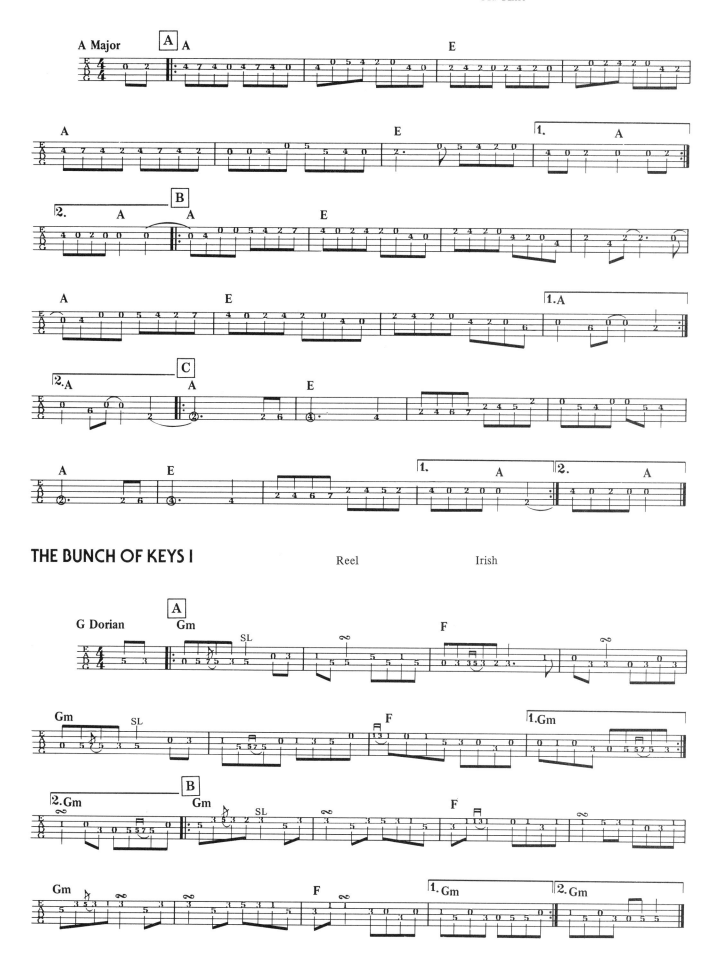

THE BUNCH OF KEYS I

Reel   Irish

BUNCH OF KEYS II

Old-Time

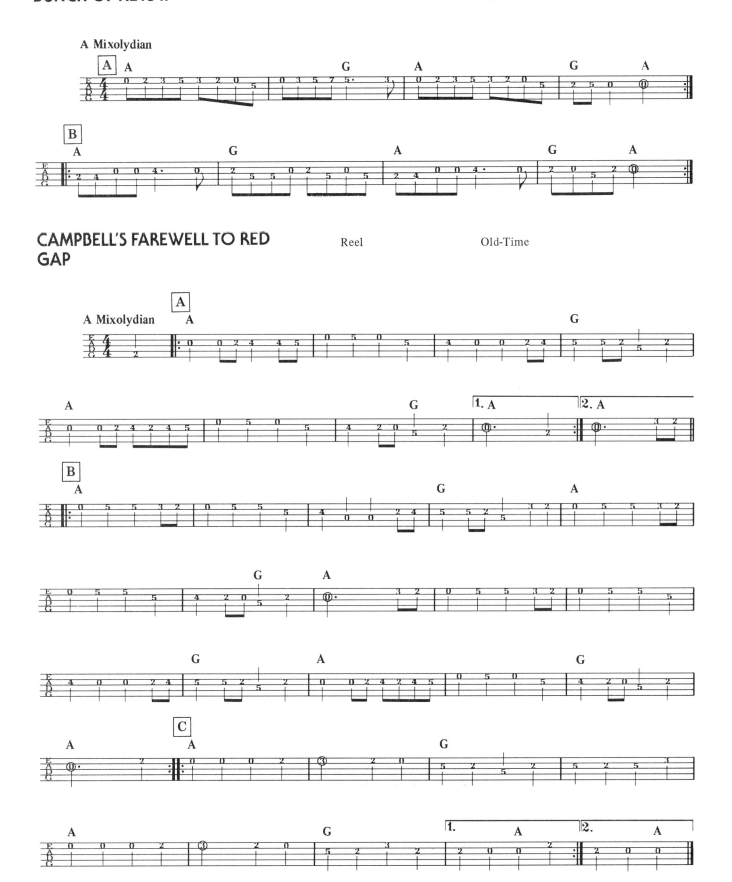

CAMPBELL'S FAREWELL TO RED GAP

Reel   Old-Time

CAROLAN'S CONCERTO

by Turlough O'Carolan   Irish

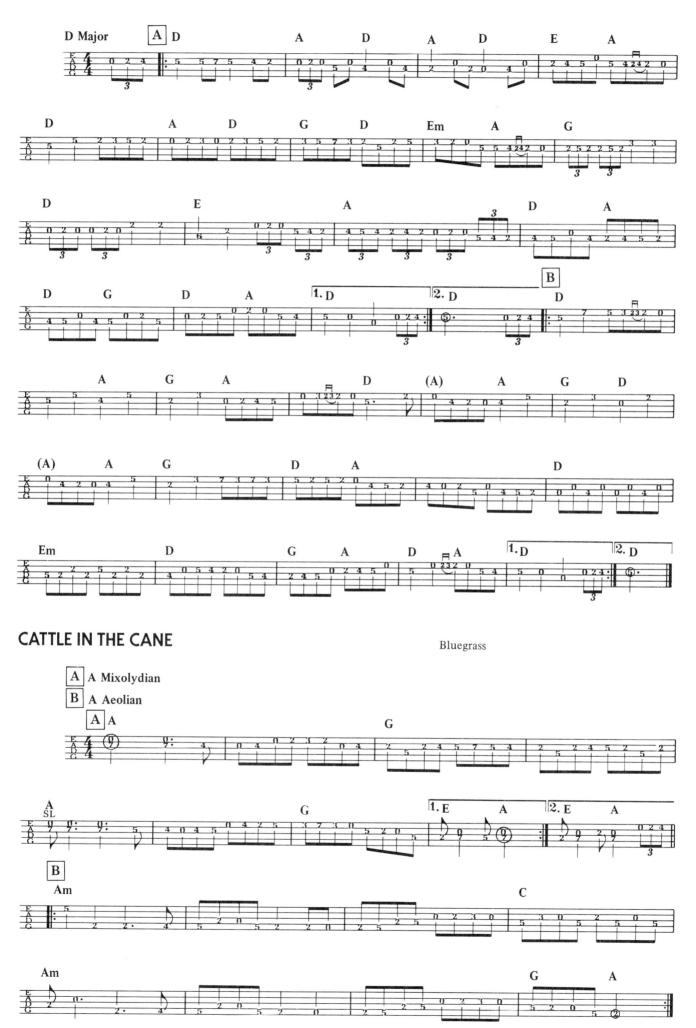

CATTLE IN THE CANE

Bluegrass

CHEROKEE SHUFFLE

Old-Time

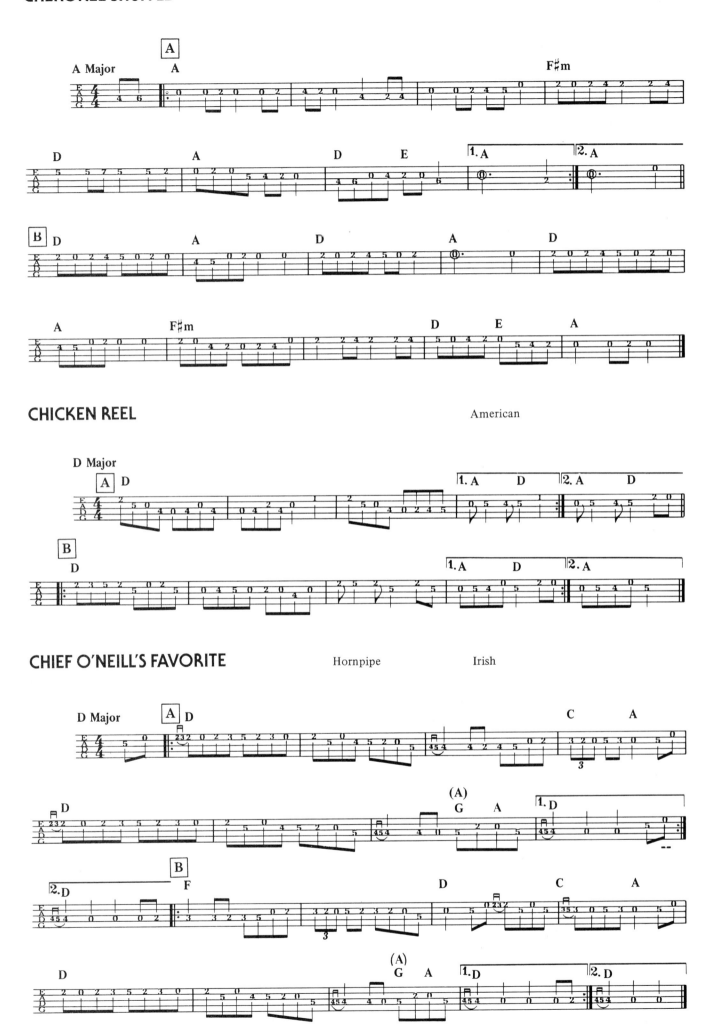

CHICKEN REEL

American

CHIEF O'NEILL'S FAVORITE

Hornpipe   Irish

CHORUS JIG

Reel   British Isles, New England

This tune is often played A A C B ending either on an A or a B part.

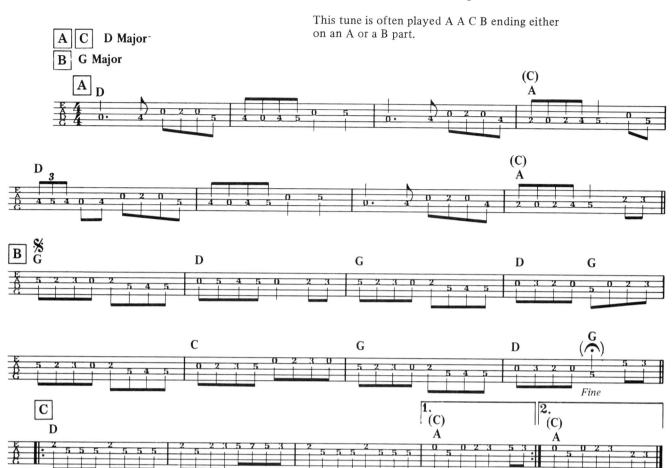

CLUCK OLD HEN

Old-Time

A Minor can be substituted for A Major in the B part.

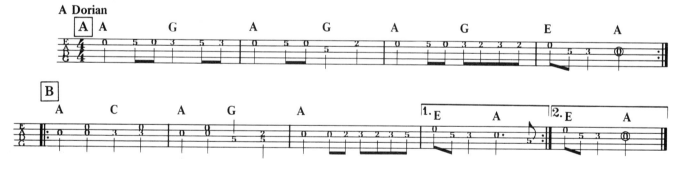

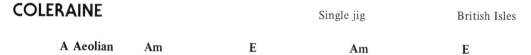

COLERAINE

Single jig   British Isles

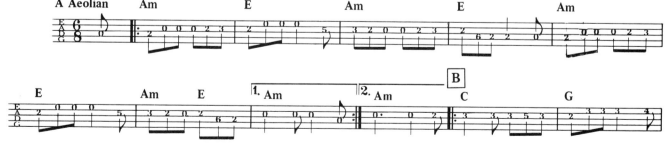

COLORED ARISTOCRACY

Old-Time, New England

COME DANCE AND SING

Reel   New England

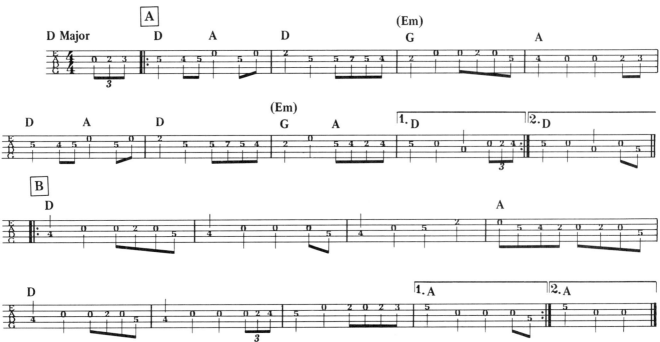

THE CONGRESS REEL

Irish

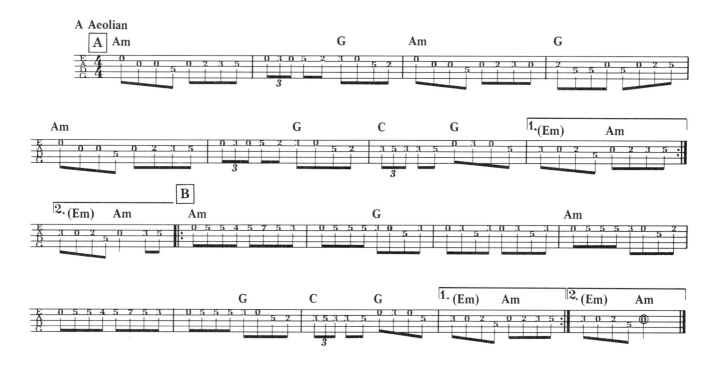

COOLEY'S REEL

Irish

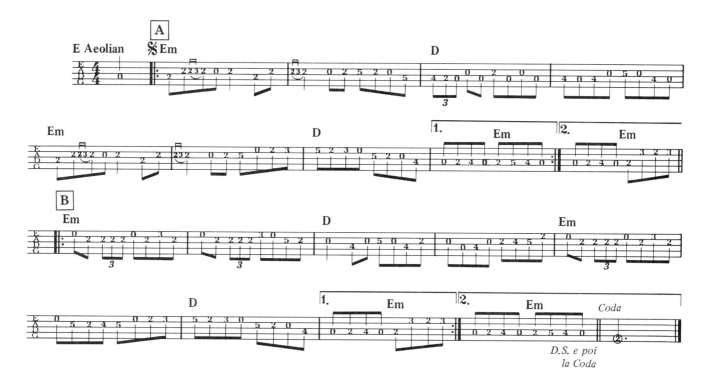

COTTON PATCH RAG

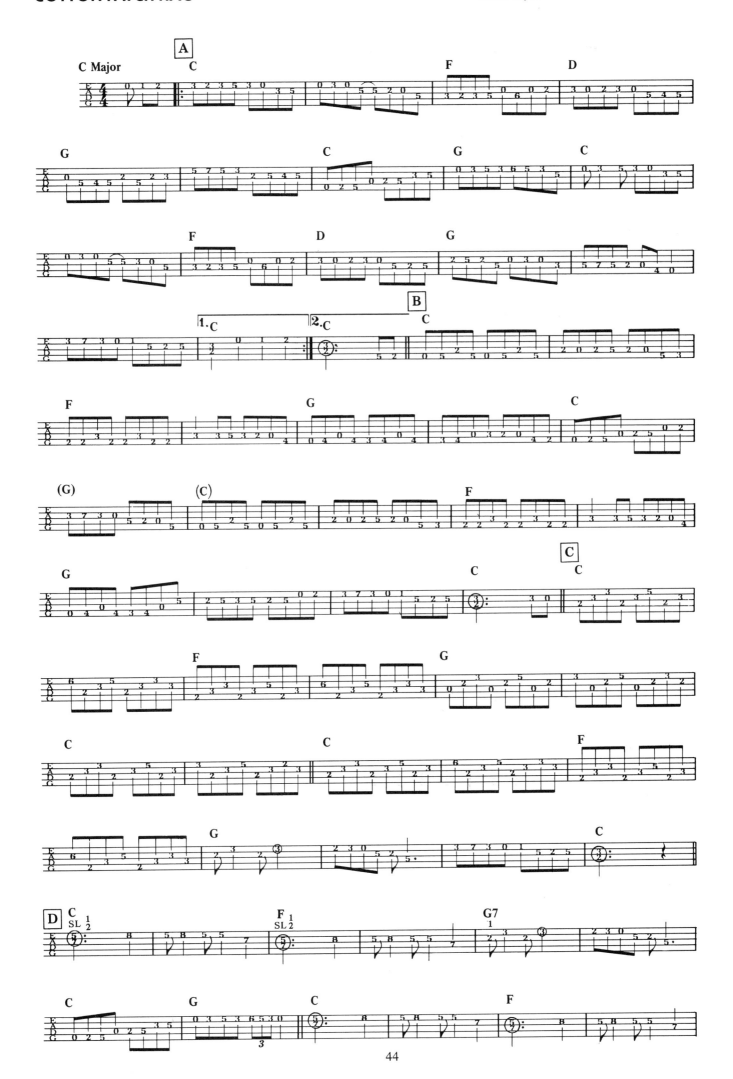

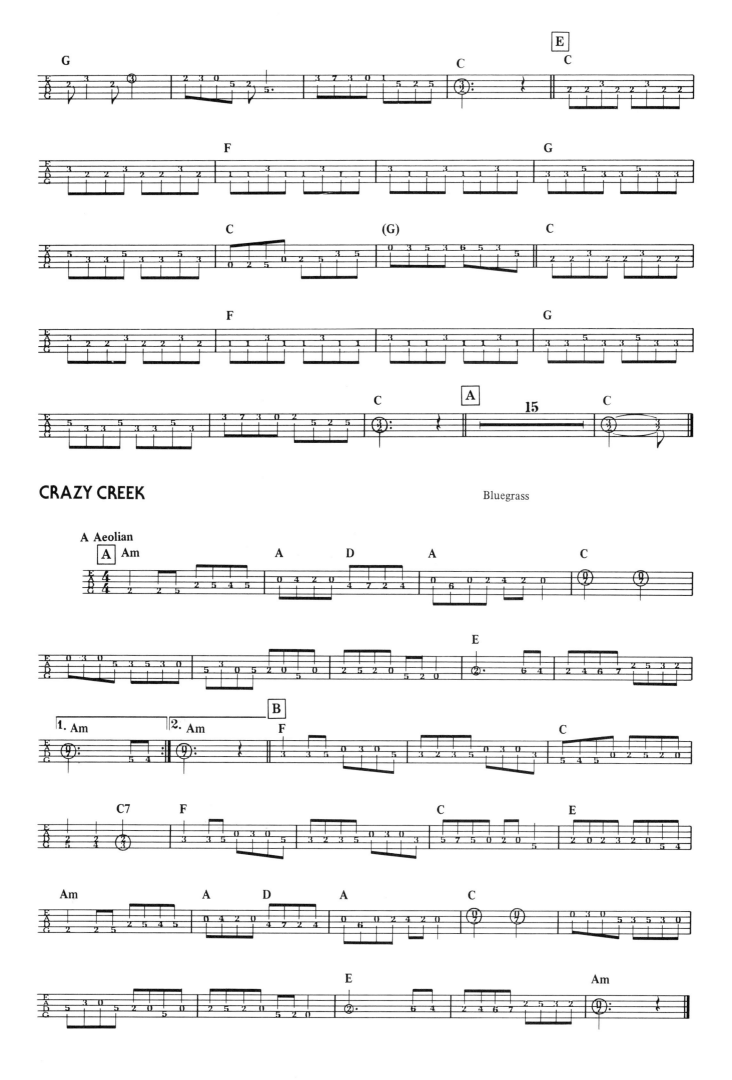

CRAZY CREEK

Bluegrass

CRICKET ON THE HEARTH

Old-Time, Bluegrass

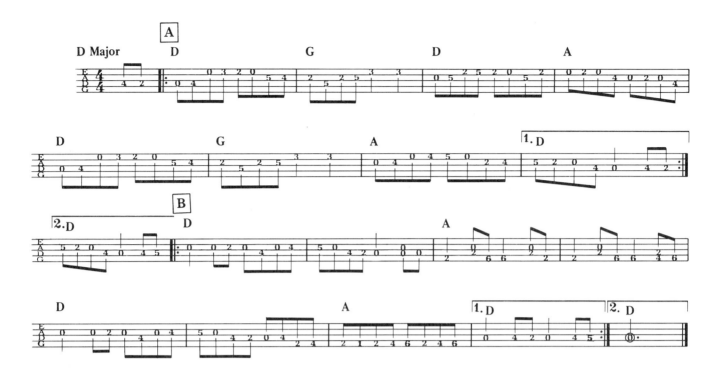

CRIPPLE CREEK 2

Bluegrass

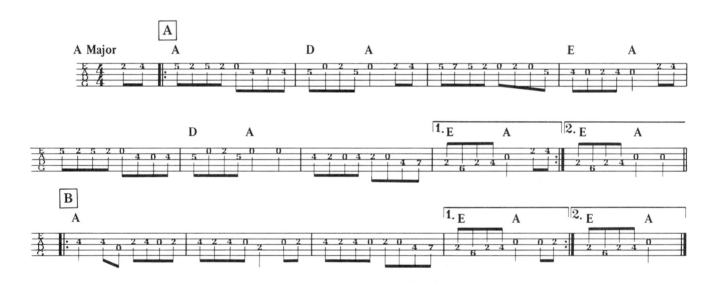

CROSS REEL

Shetland

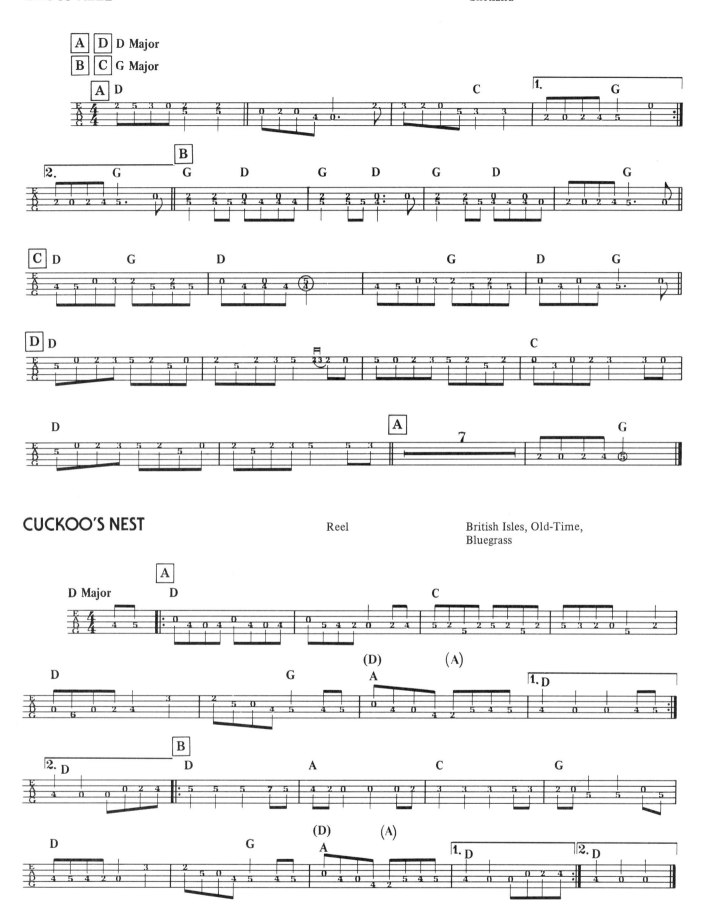

CUCKOO'S NEST

Reel

British Isles, Old-Time,
Bluegrass

CUFFEY

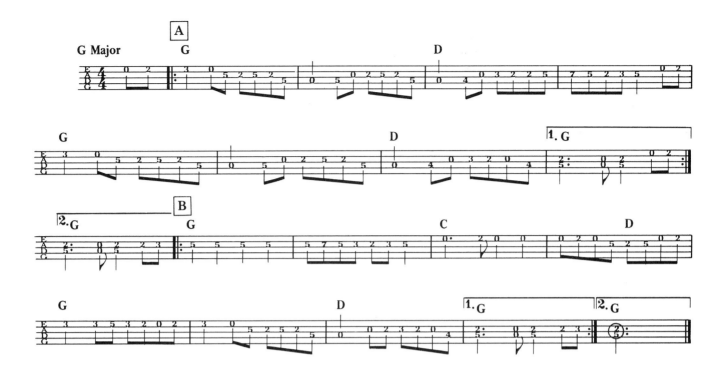

DAILEY'S REEL

Old-Time, Bluegrass

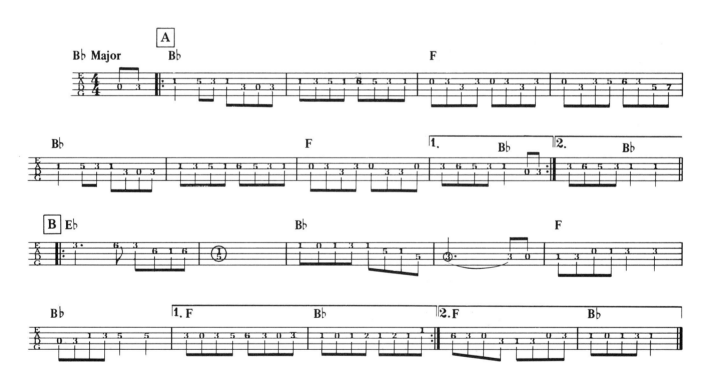

DALLAS RAG

Country rag   Old-Time

DANCE ALL NIGHT

Old-Time

Some musicians play this as a three-part tune using the following as a C part. If this is done the tune is played AABAACCB.

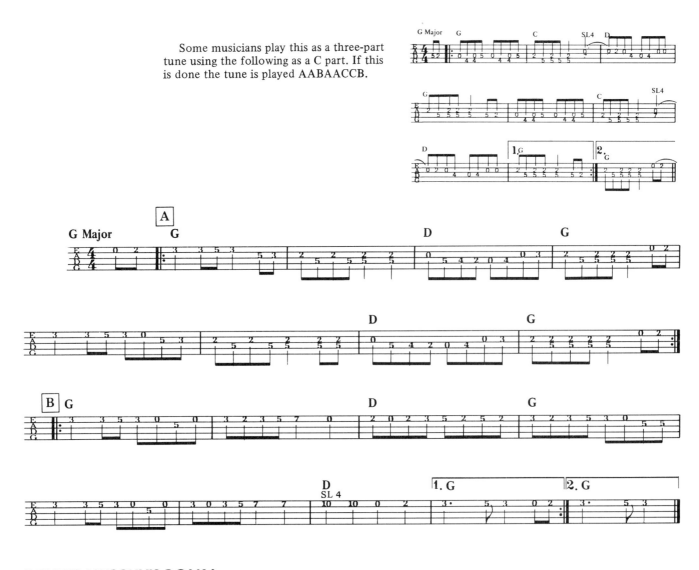

DENNIS MURPHY'S POLKA

Irish

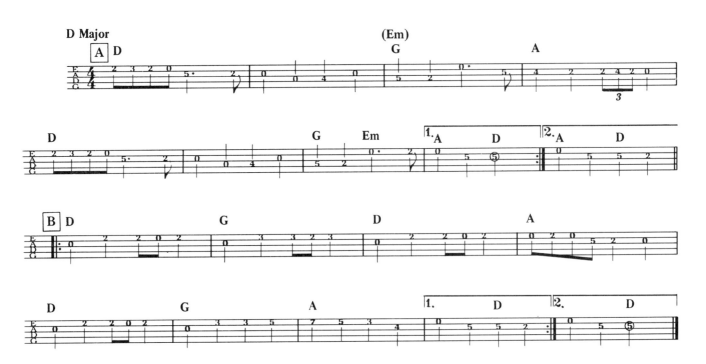

DEVIL'S DREAM

Reel   British Isles, North American

DILL PICKLE RAG

Novelty rag
by Charles L. Johnson   Old-Time, Texas Style

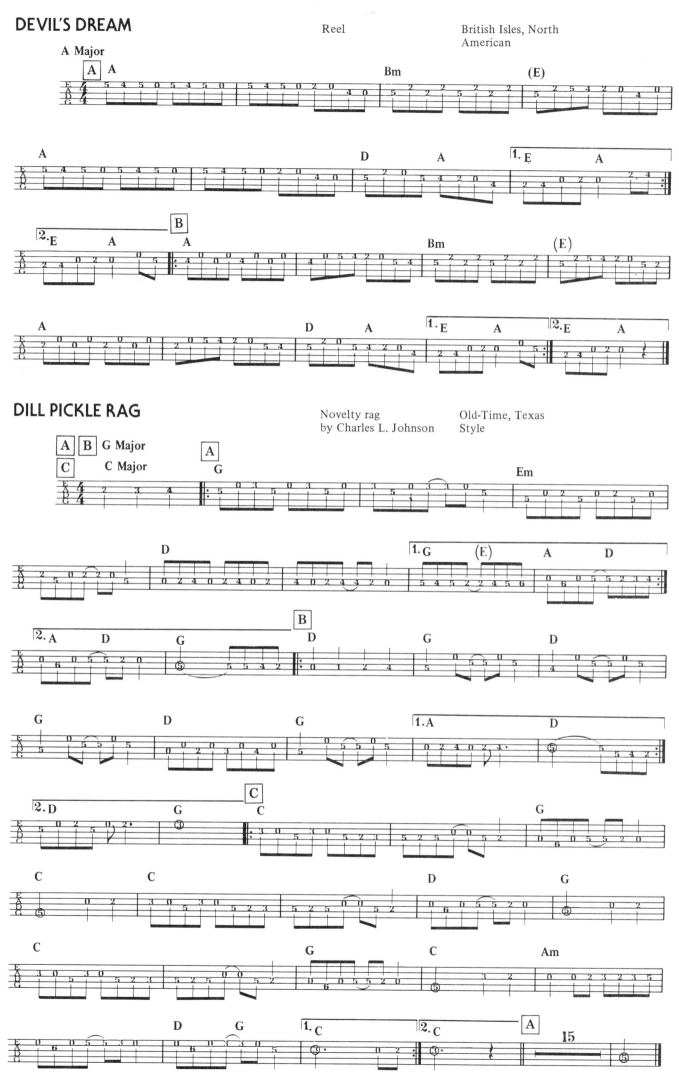

DONE GONE

Old-Time, Bluegrass

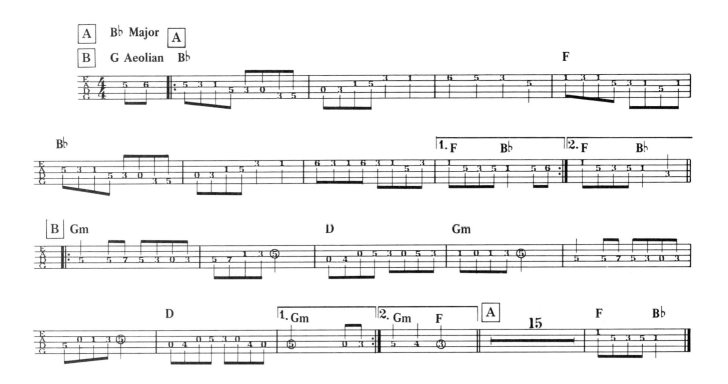

DON TREMAINE'S REEL

New England

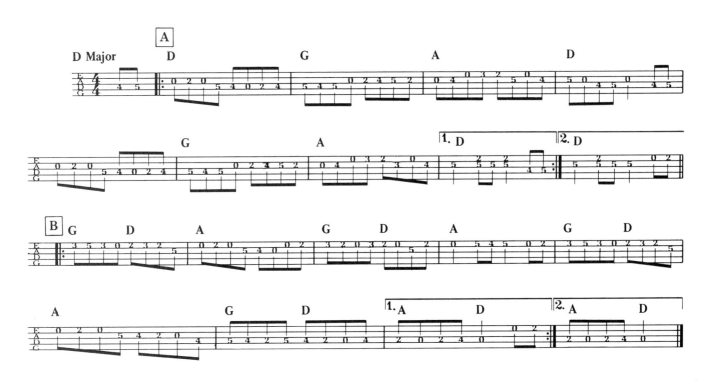

DOUBLE FILE

Old-Time

DOWD'S FAVORITE

Reel   Irish

DRAGGIN' THE BOW

Western Swing

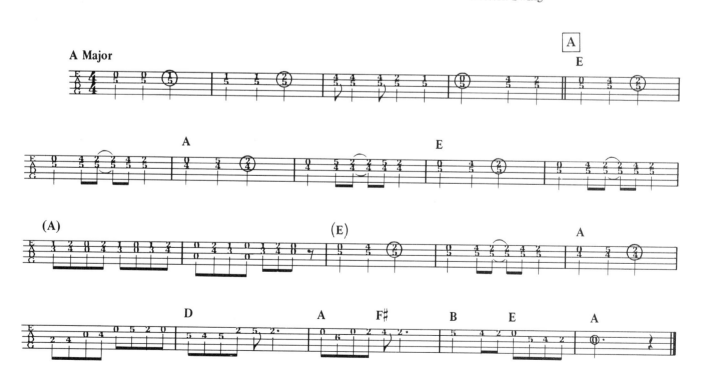

DROWSY MAGGIE

Irish

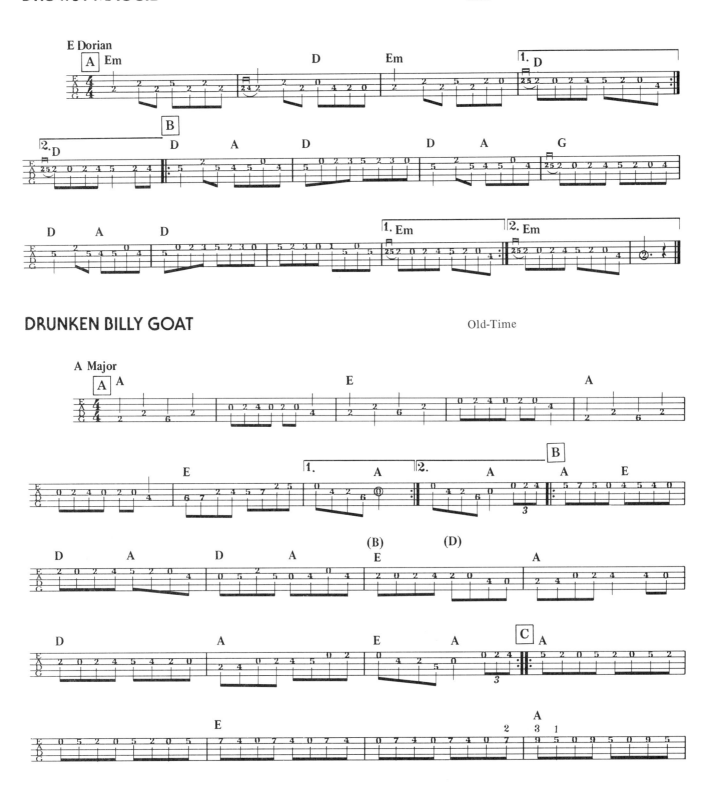

DRUNKEN BILLY GOAT

Old-Time

DUBUQUE

Reel   New England

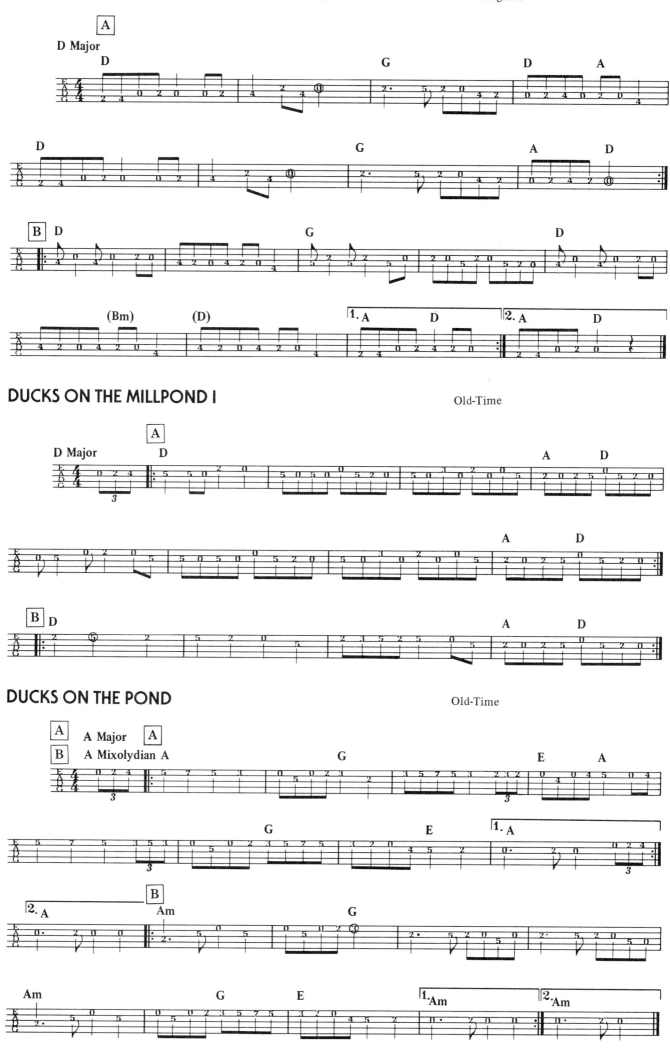

DUCKS ON THE MILLPOND I

Old-Time

DUCKS ON THE POND

Old-Time

DURANG'S HORNPIPE 1

Old-Time, New England

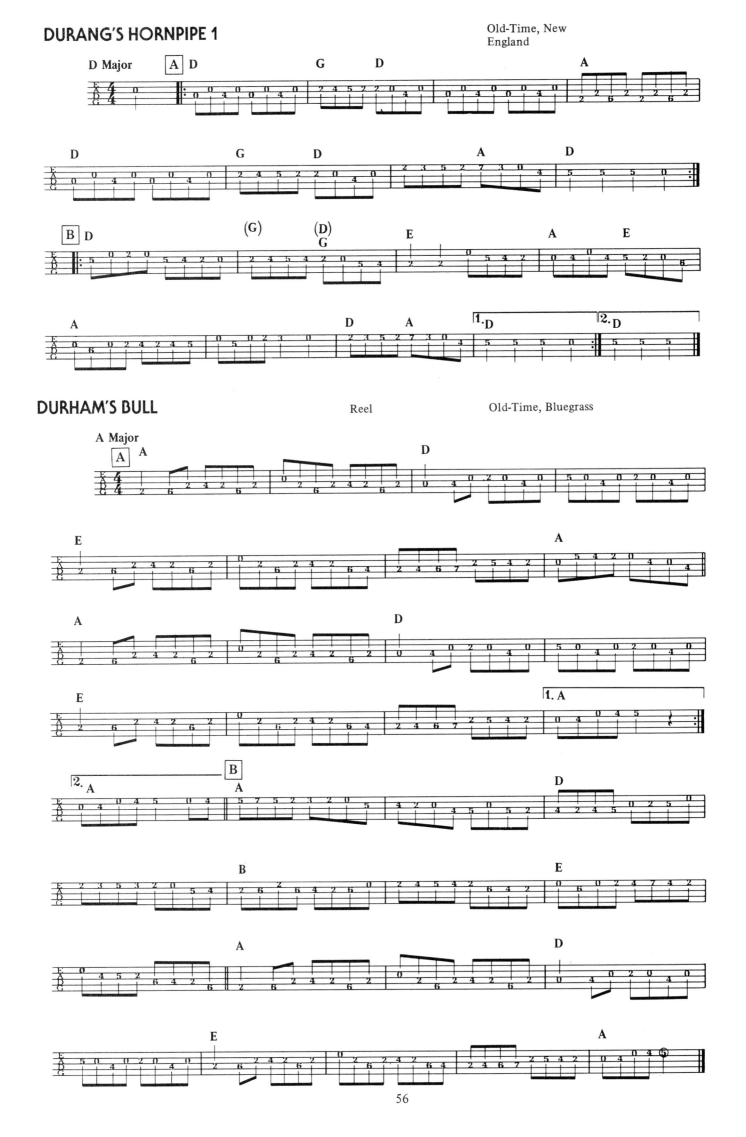

DURHAM'S BULL

Reel   Old-Time, Bluegrass

56

DUSTY MILLER I

Old-Time

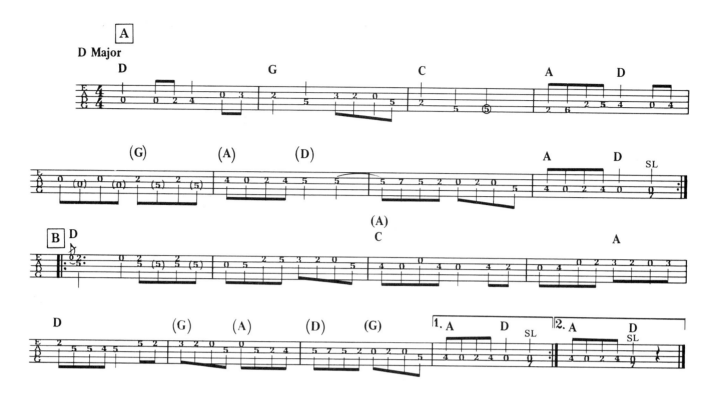

DUSTY MILLER II B

Bluegrass, Texas
Style

Some musicians begin on what is here the C
part, following with the A and B parts.

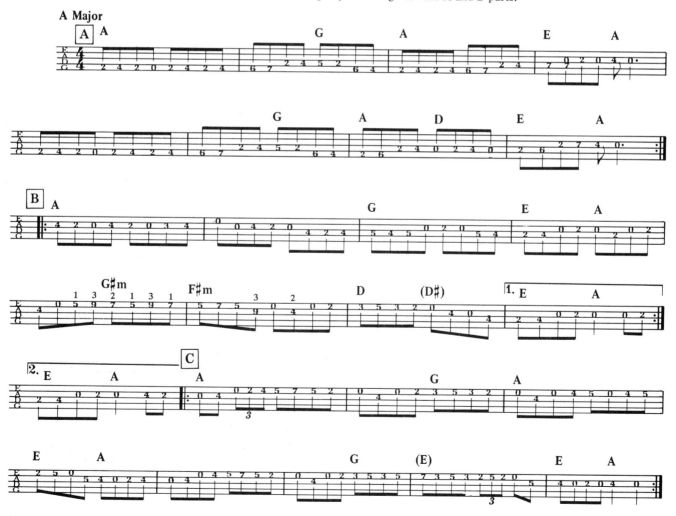

EAST TENNESSEE BLUES

Old-Time, Bluegrass

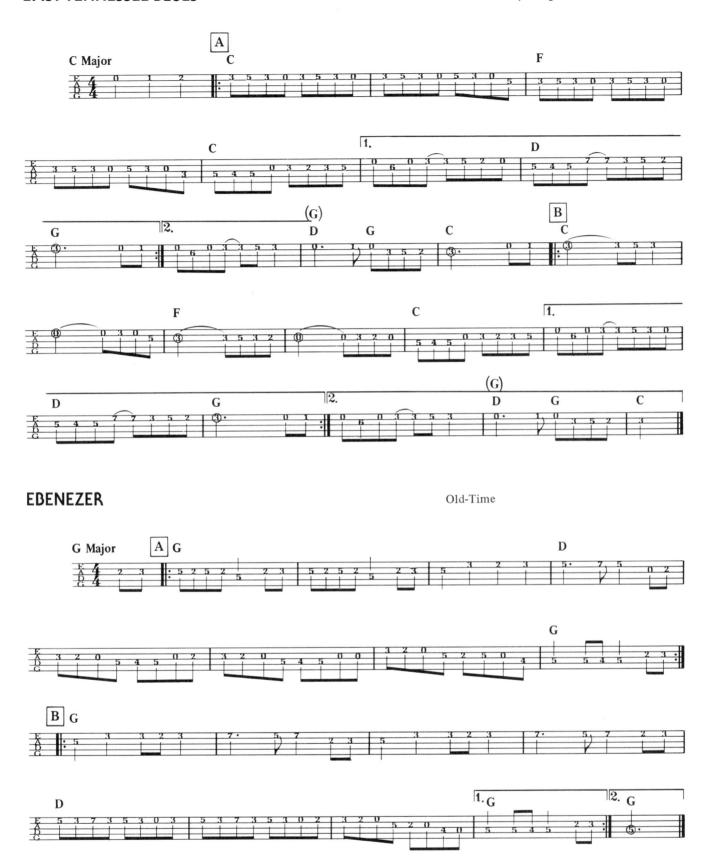

EBENEZER

Old-Time

EIGHTH OF JANUARY

Old-Time, Bluegrass

ELZIC'S FAREWELL

Old-Time

Some musicians play the following as an A part. If this is done the parts marked A and B are played as B and C parts and the part marked C is not played.

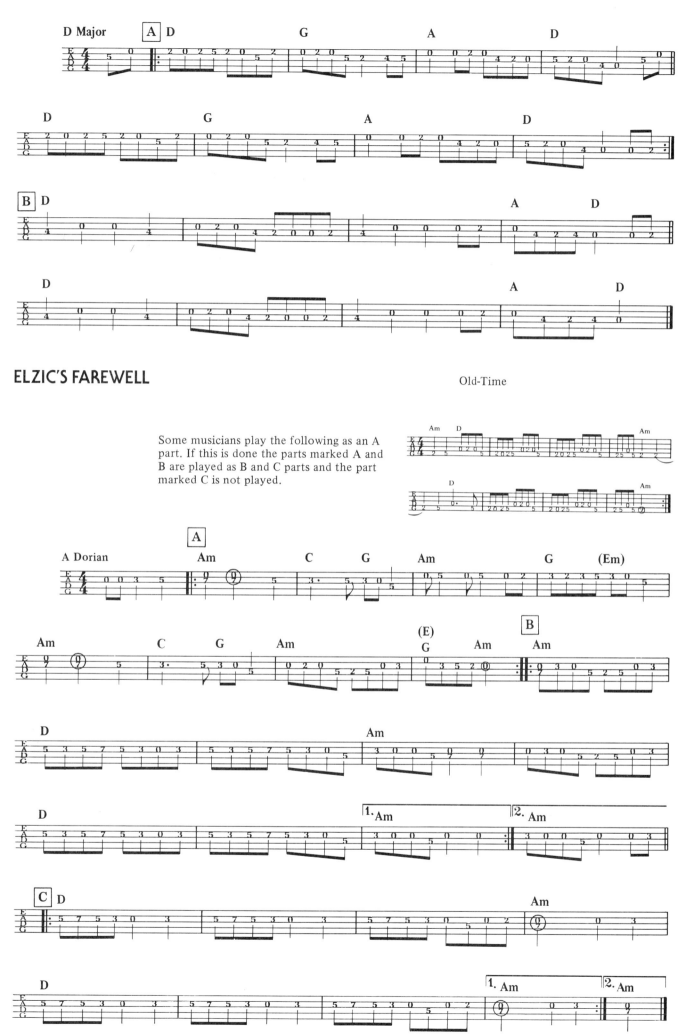

FAIRY DANCE

Reel   Irish

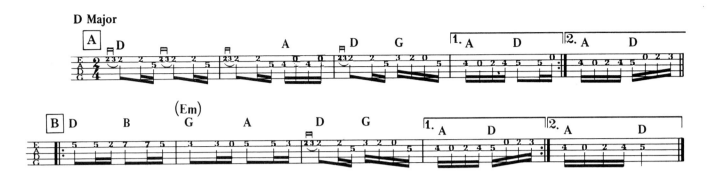

FIRE ON THE MOUNTAIN

Old-Time, Bluegrass

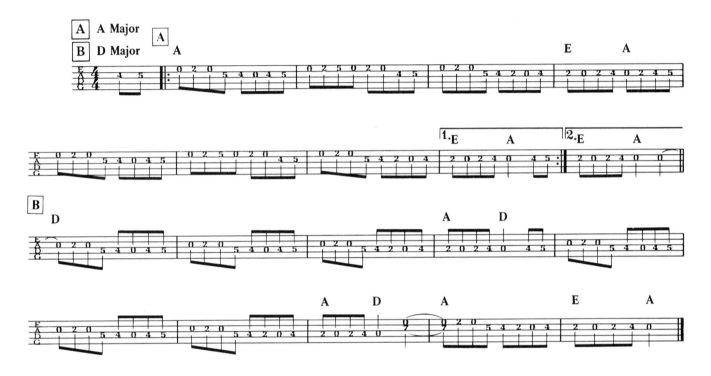

FISHER'S HORNPIPE

British Isles, North American

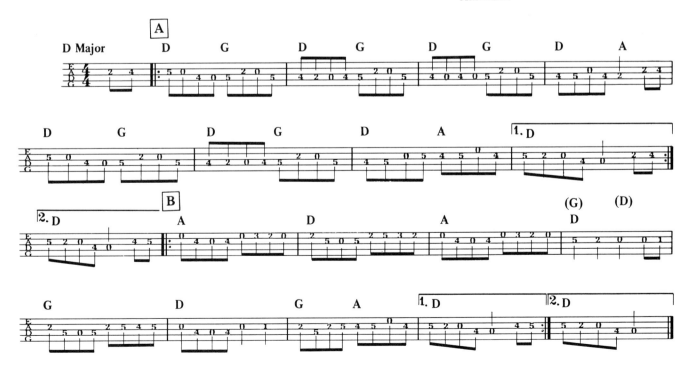

FLOP-EARED MULE

Old-Time, Bluegrass

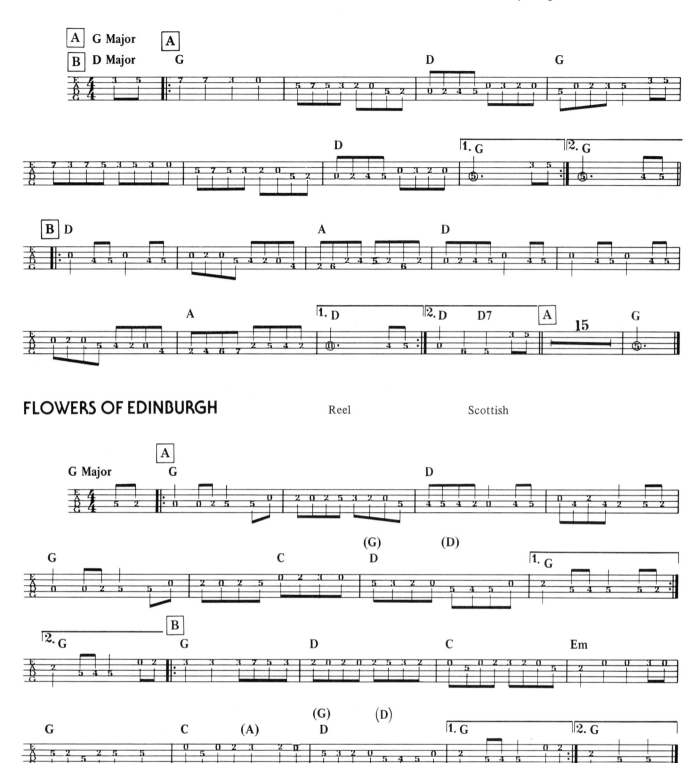

FLOWERS OF EDINBURGH

Reel   Scottish

FLYING CLOUD COTILLION

New England

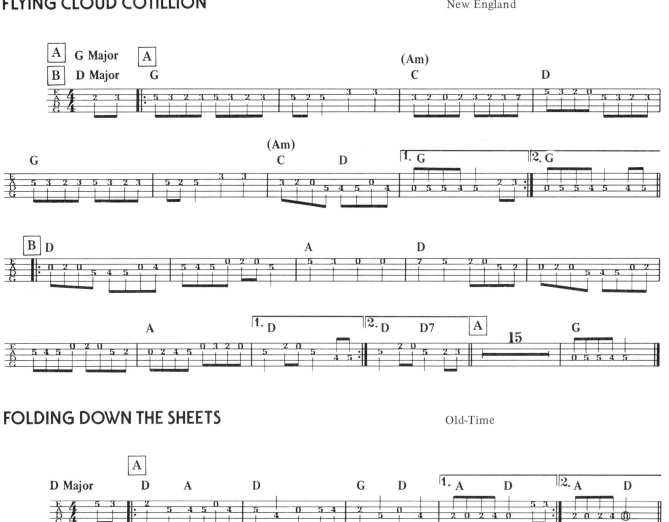

FOLDING DOWN THE SHEETS

Old-Time

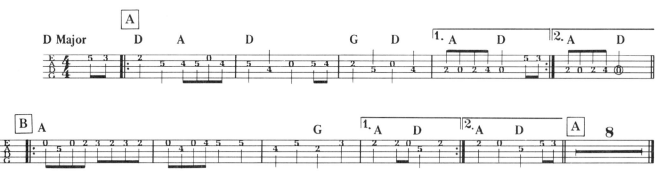

FORKED DEER

Old-Time

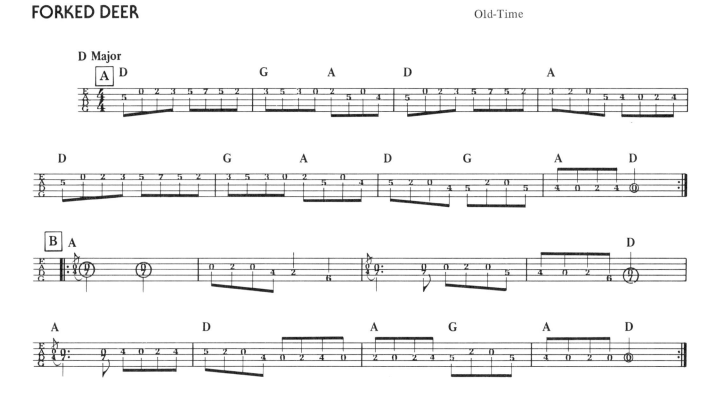

62

FRIEZE BREECHES

Double jig   Irish

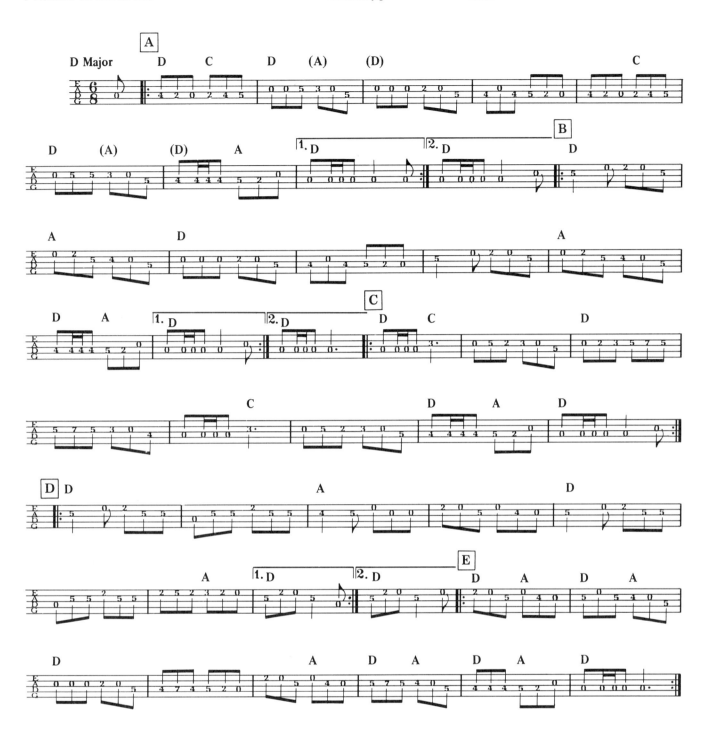

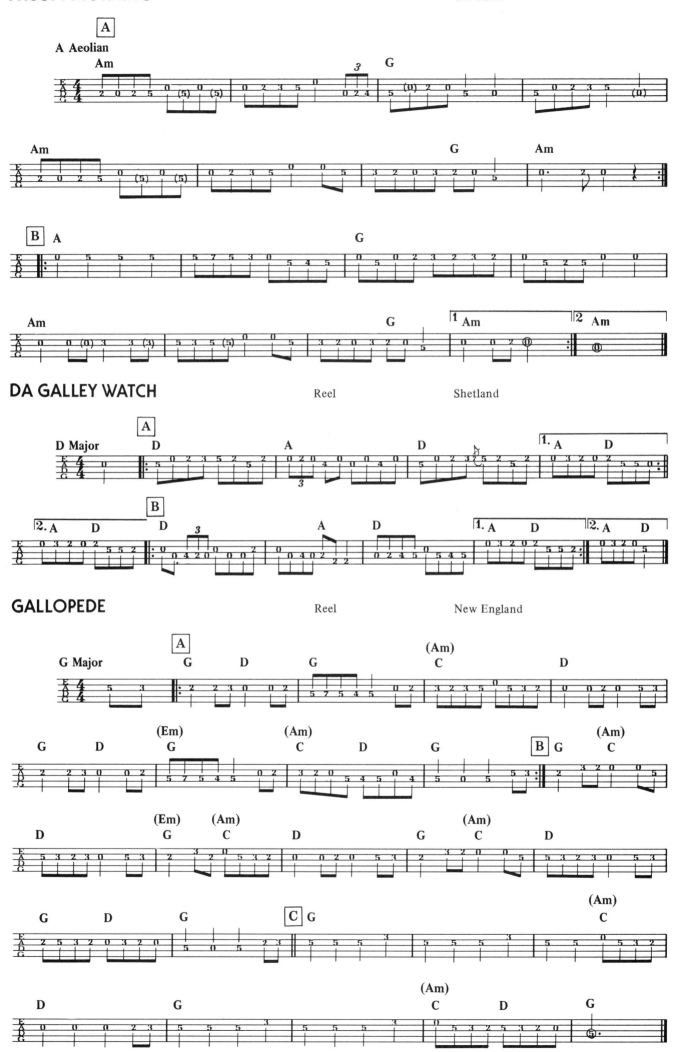

GASPÉ REEL

French Canadian

This tune ends on the B part.

THE GIRL I LEFT BEHIND ME

Old-Time, New England

65

GIVE THE FIDDLER A DRAM I

Old-Time

A *2* (F♯) with an asterisk above it may be
played as a *1* (F♮).

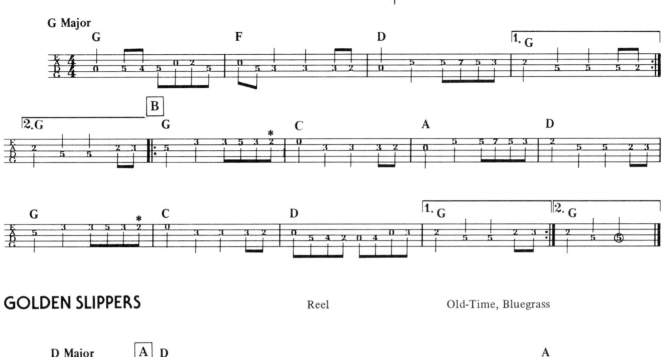

GOLDEN SLIPPERS

Reel   Old-Time, Bluegrass

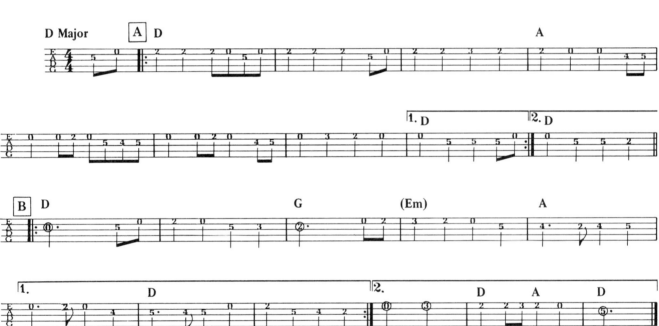

THE GOLD RING

Double jig   Irish

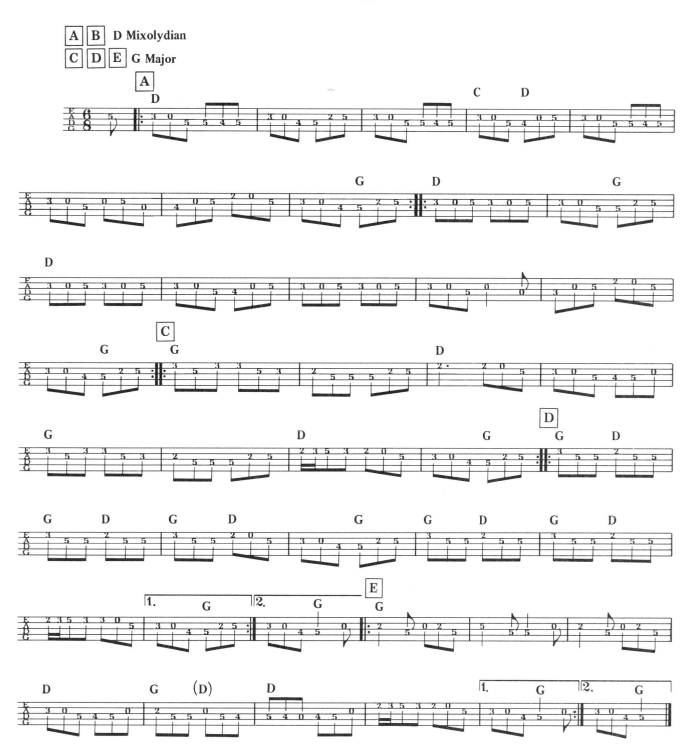

GOODBYE LIZA JANE

Old-Time, Bluegrass,
Western Swing

THE GRAVEL WALK

Reel   Irish

GREENFIELDS OF AMERICA

Reel   Irish

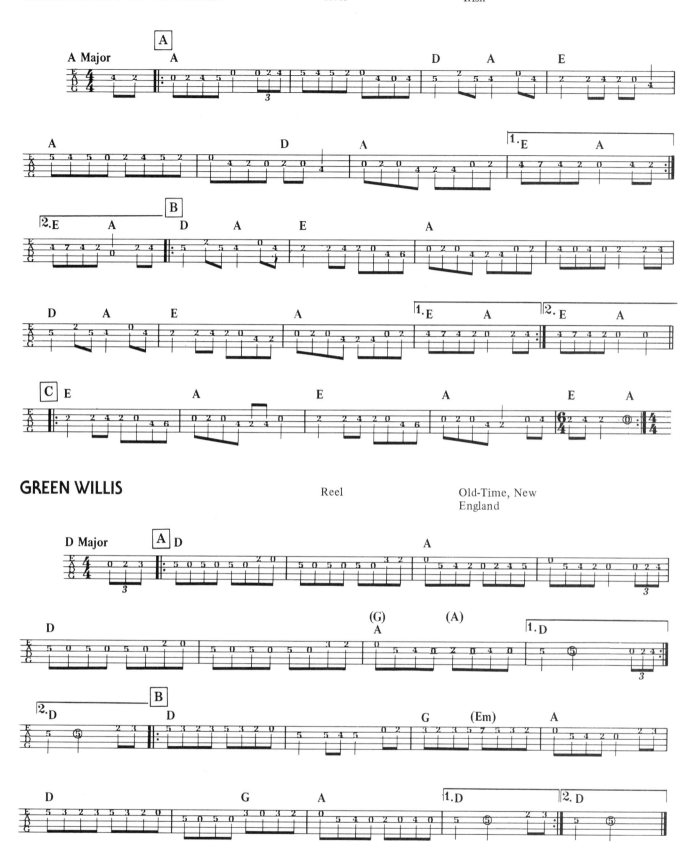

GREEN WILLIS

Reel   Old-Time, New
England

GREY EAGLE

Old-Time, Bluegrass

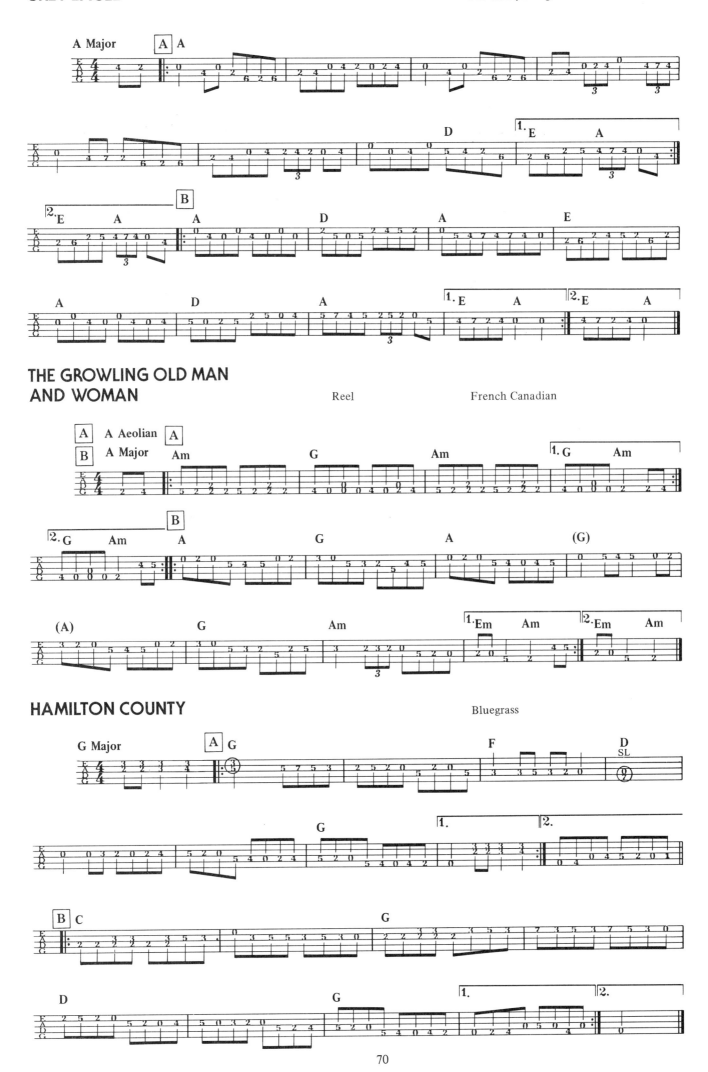

THE GROWLING OLD MAN
AND WOMAN

Reel   French Canadian

HAMILTON COUNTY

Bluegrass

HARVEST HOME

Hornpipe

British Isles, New England

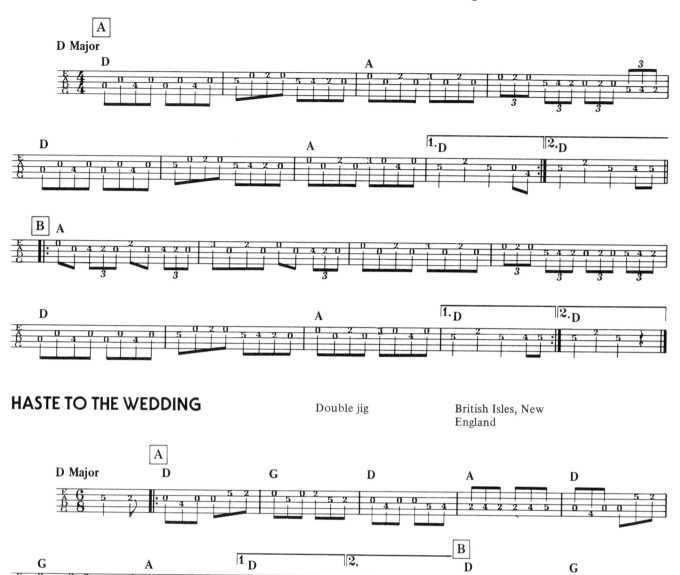

HASTE TO THE WEDDING

Double jig

British Isles, New England

HAWKINS' RAG

Country rag
by Ted Hawkins

Old-Time

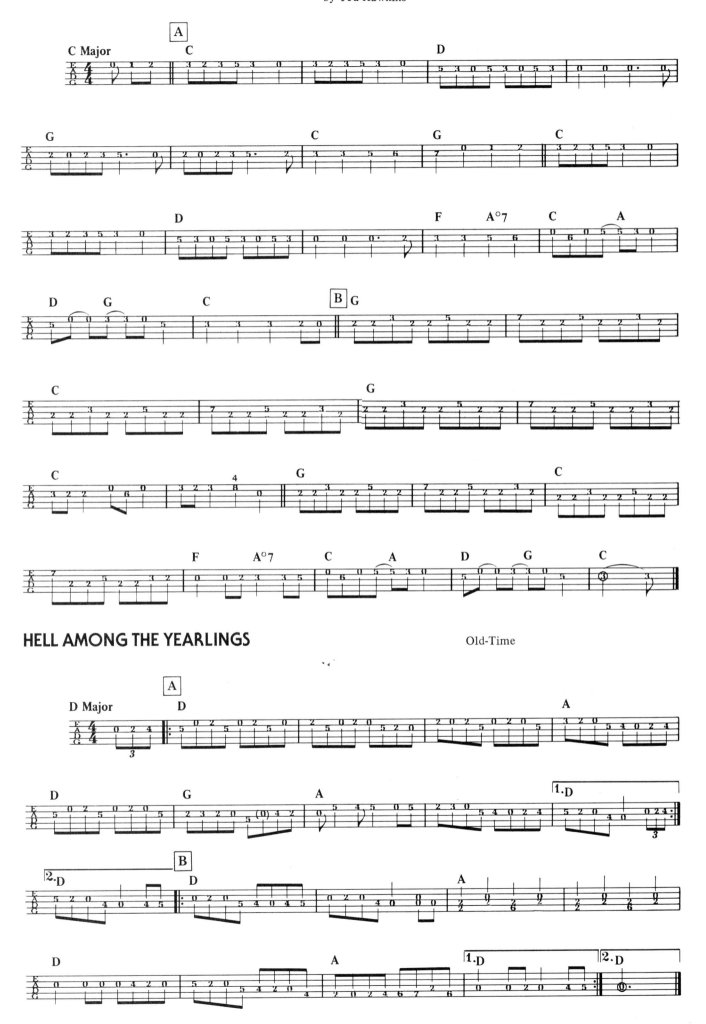

HELL AMONG THE YEARLINGS

Old-Time

HOG EYE

Old-Time

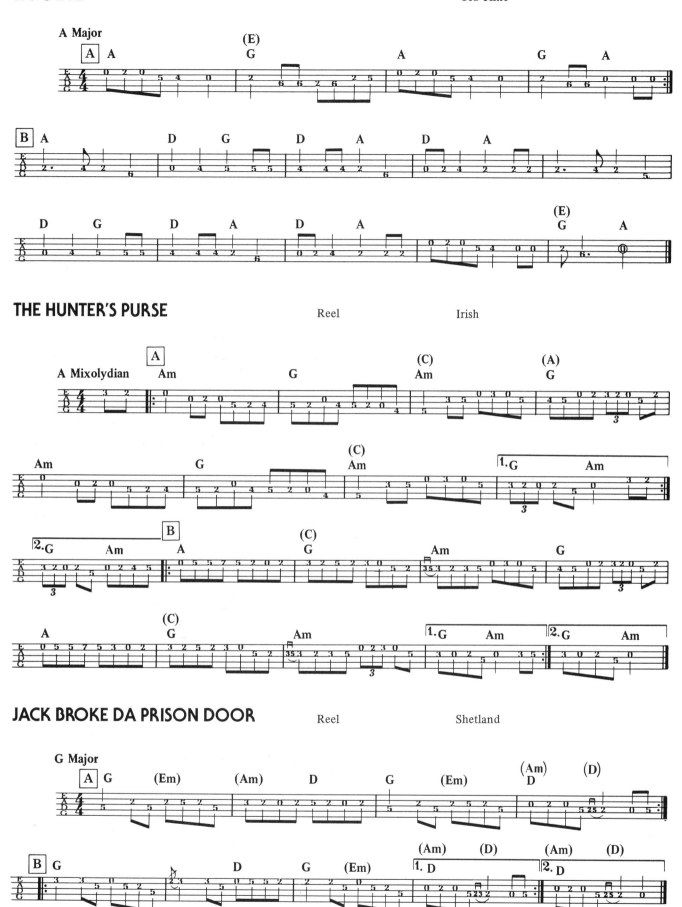

THE HUNTER'S PURSE

Reel   Irish

JACK BROKE DA PRISON DOOR

Reel   Shetland

JACKSON STOMP

Old-Time

A Major

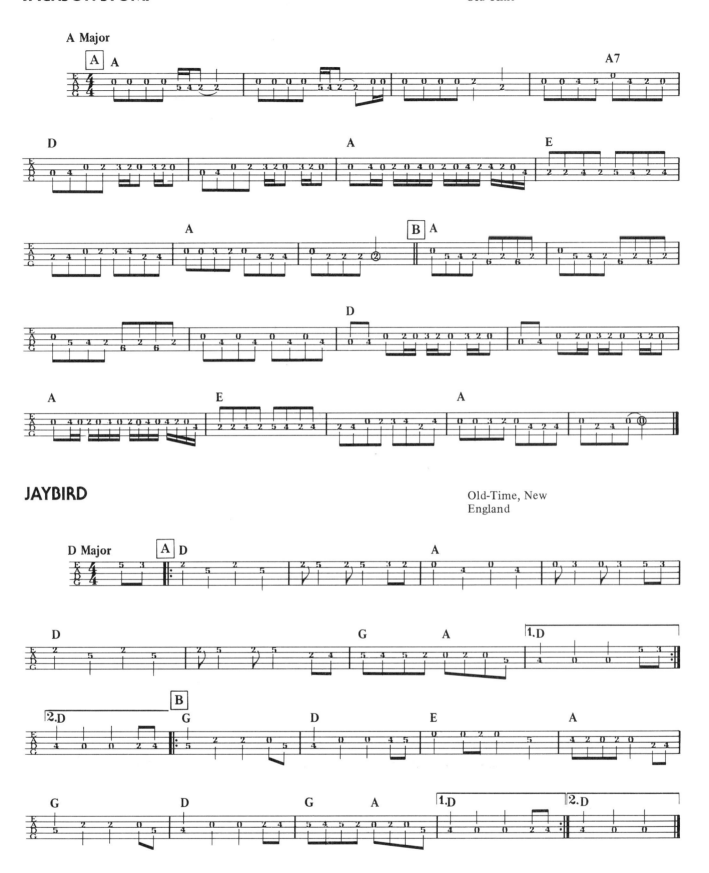

JAYBIRD

Old-Time, New
England

D Major

74

JENNY LIND POLKA

Old-Time

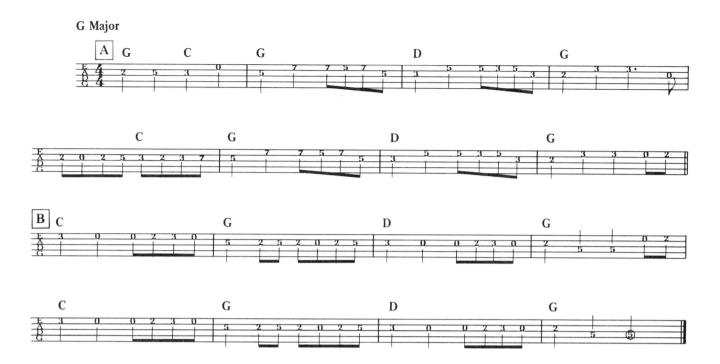

JOHNNY THE BLACKSMITH I

Bluegrass

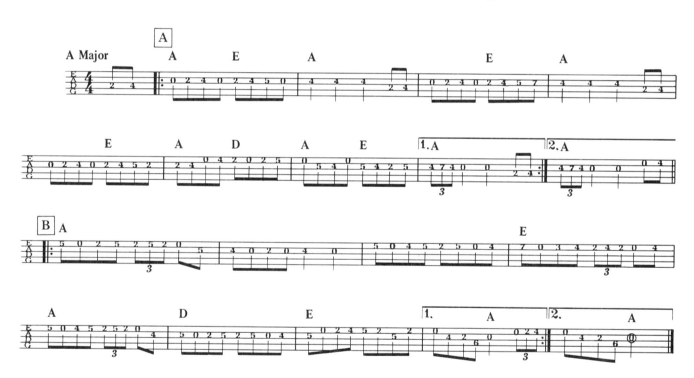

JOHN RYAN'S POLKA

Irish

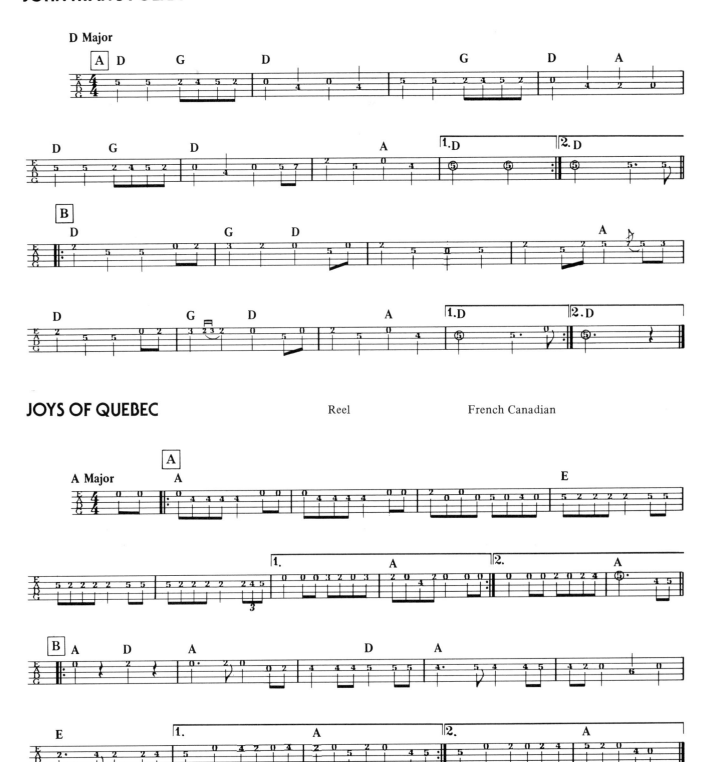

JOYS OF QUEBEC

Reel   French Canadian

JUNE APPLE

Old-Time

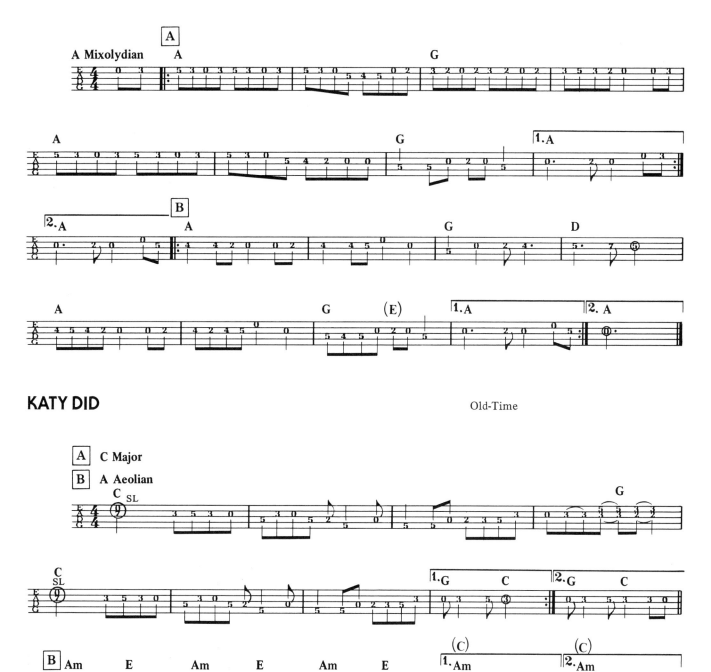

KATY DID

Old-Time

KATY HILL

Old-Time, Bluegrass

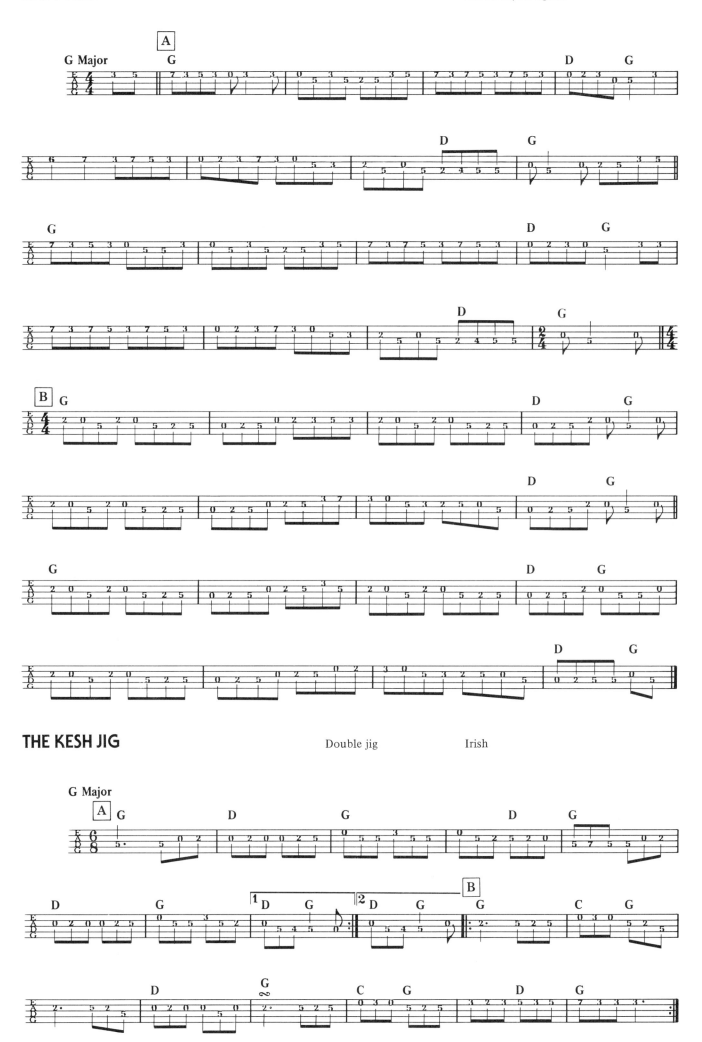

THE KESH JIG

Double jig   Irish

THE KING OF THE FAIRIES

Irish

THE KITCHEN GIRL

Old-Time

A *4* (C♯) with an asterisk above it may be
played as a *3* (C♮). If this is done the accompanying chord will be an A Minor.

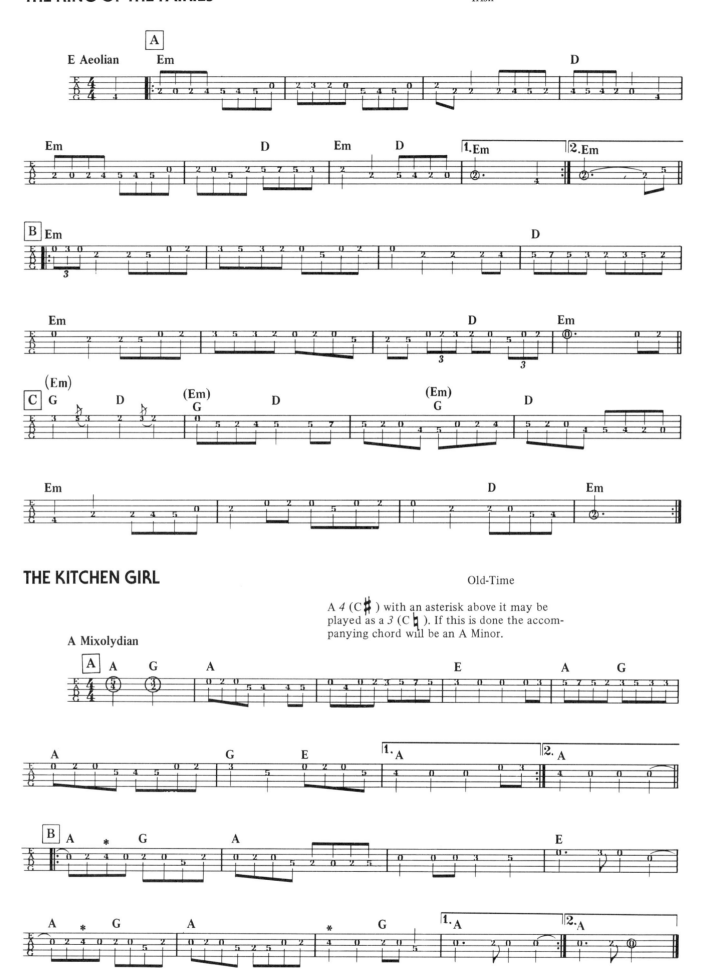

THE LARK IN THE MORNING

Double jig   Irish

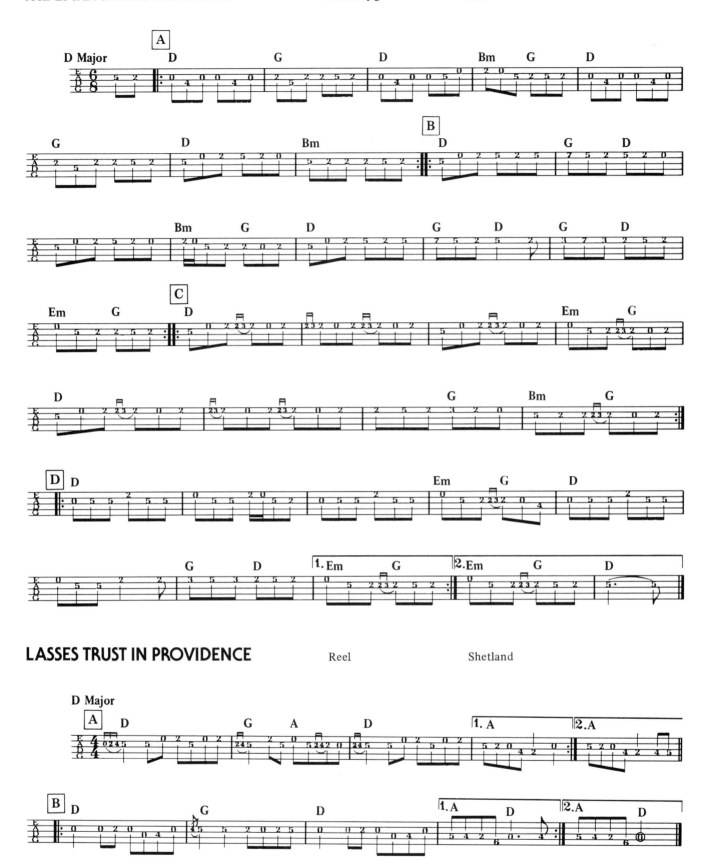

LASSES TRUST IN PROVIDENCE

Reel   Shetland

THE LAST OF CALLAHAN

Old-Time

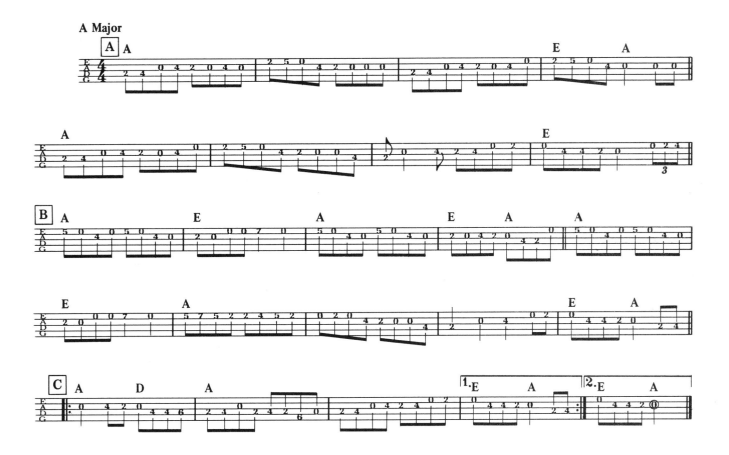

LEATHER BRITCHES

Old-Time, Bluegrass

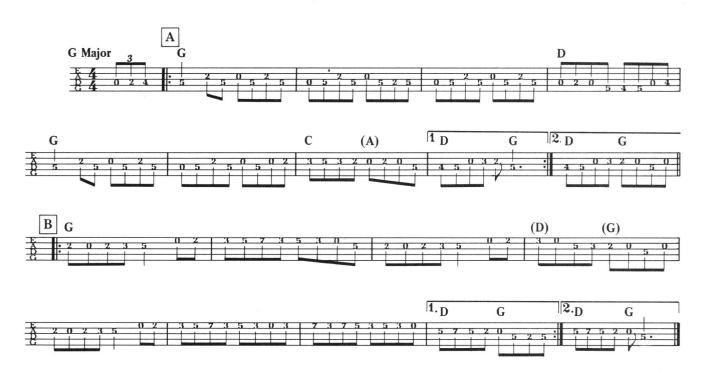

LEE HIGHWAY BLUES

Old-Time, Bluegrass

DA LERWICKS LASSES

Reel   Shetland

LIBERTY

Old-Time, Bluegrass

LITTLE LIZA JANE

Old-Time

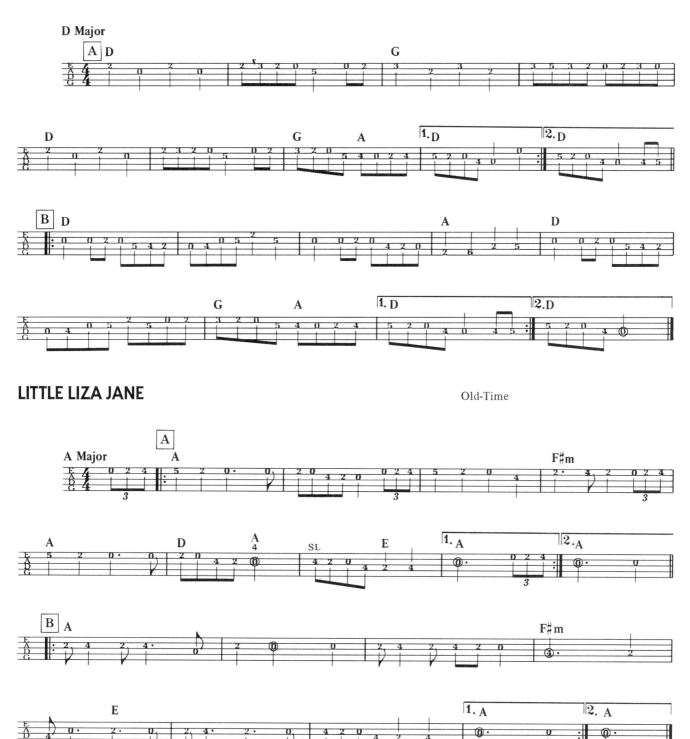

83

LITTLE RABBIT

Old-Time

LOCH LAVAN CASTLE

Old-Time, British
Isles

LORD INCHIQUIN

by Turlough O'Carolan   Irish

LOST INDIAN I

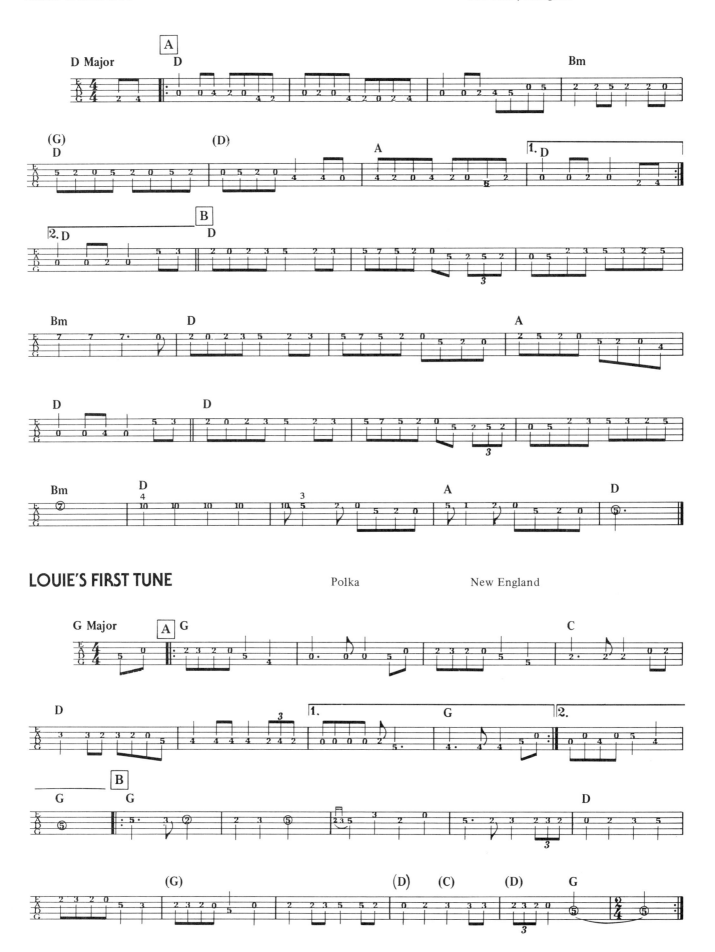

LOUIE'S FIRST TUNE

Polka   New England

MAGGIE BROWN'S FAVORITE

Single jig

Irish

by Turlough O'Carolan?

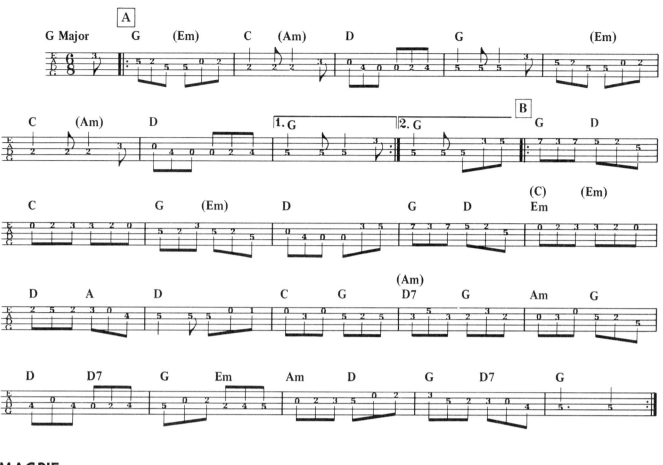

MAGPIE

Old-Time

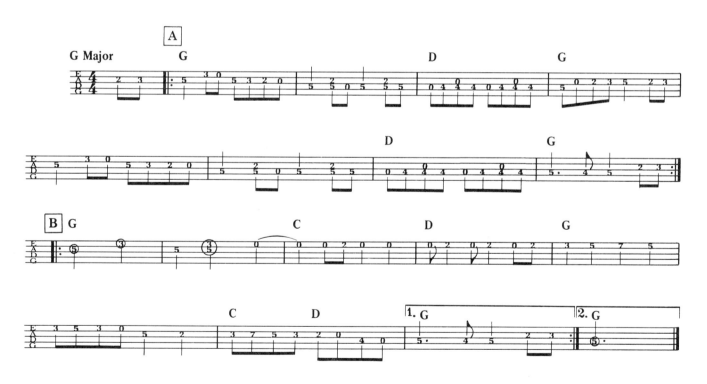

THE MAID BEHIND THE BAR

Reel   Irish

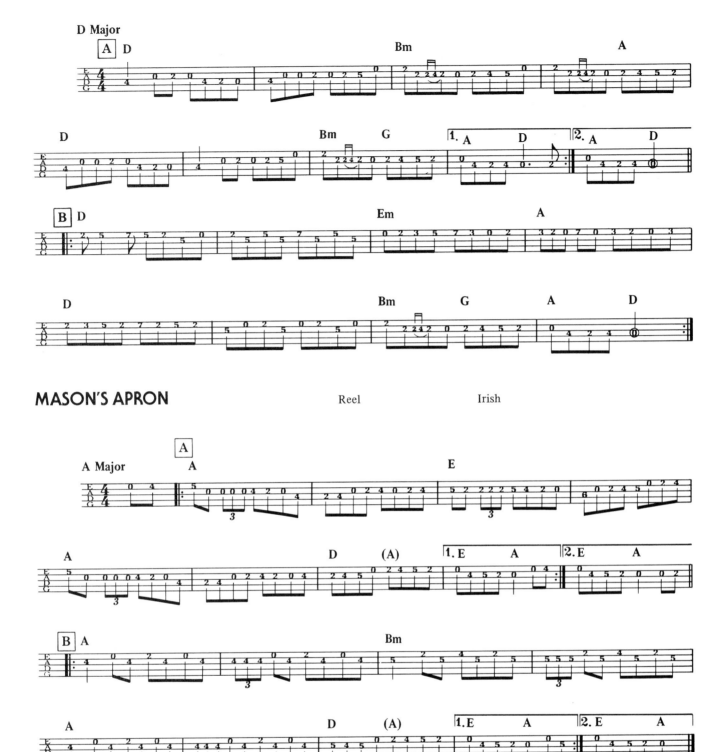

MASON'S APRON

Reel   Irish

MERRILY KISS THE QUAKER

Slide   Irish

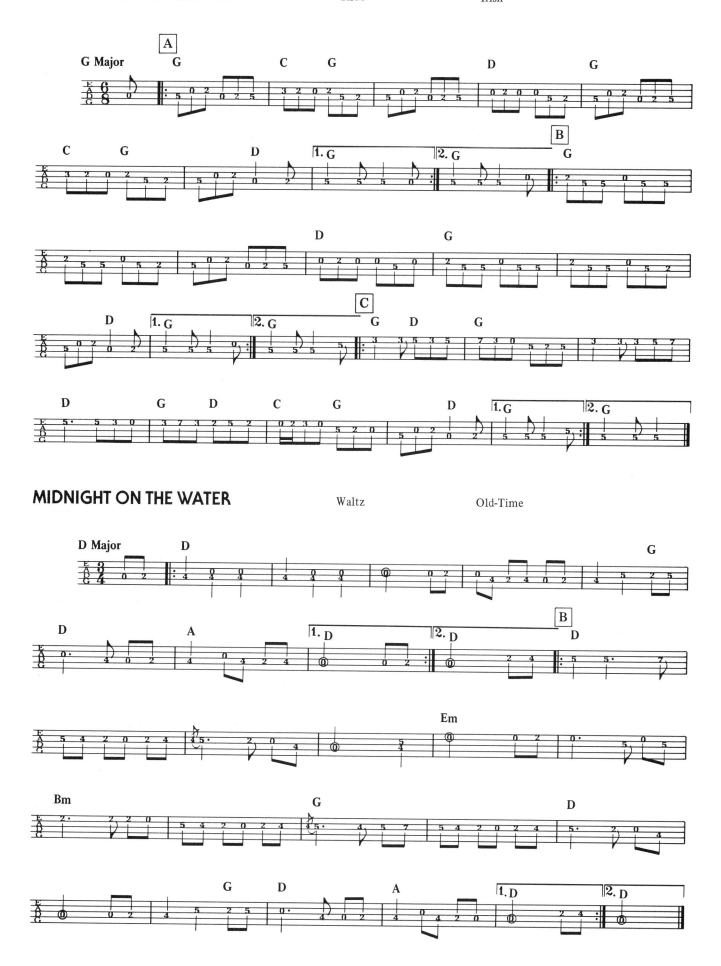

MIDNIGHT ON THE WATER

Waltz   Old-Time

MILLER'S REEL A

British Isles, American

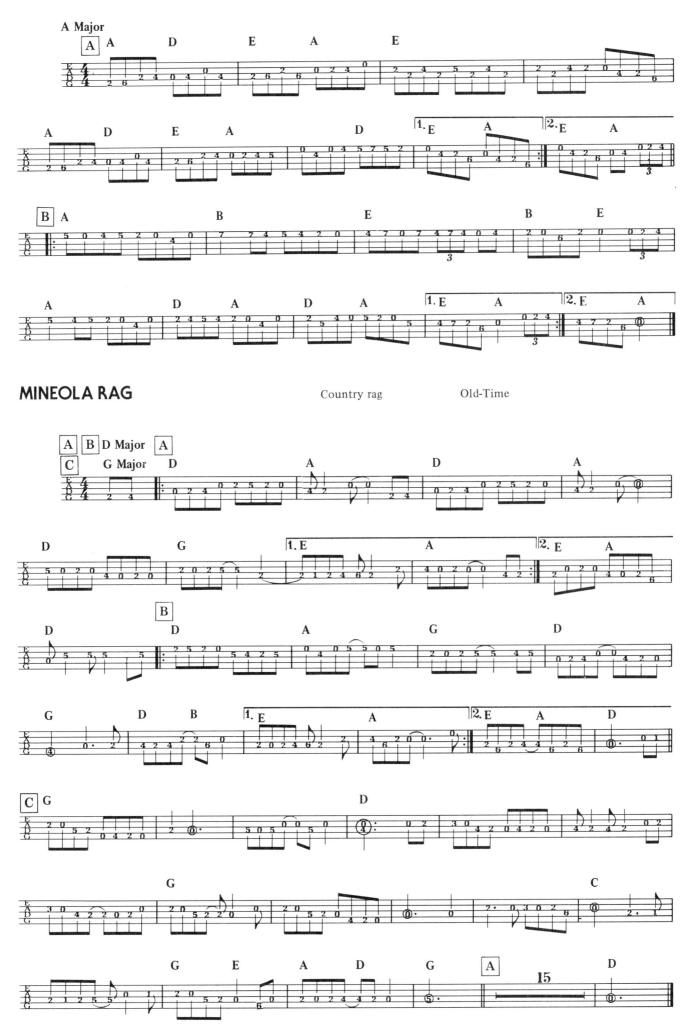

MINEOLA RAG

Country rag   Old-Time

90

MISSISSIPPI SAWYER

Old-Time

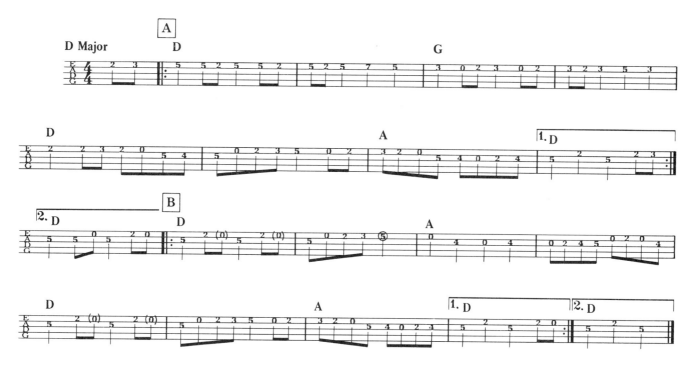

MISS McLEOD'S REEL 1

Irish

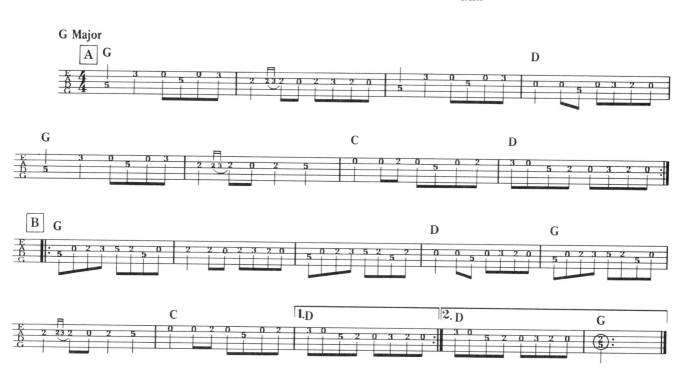

MOLLY PUT THE KETTLE ON I

Old-Time

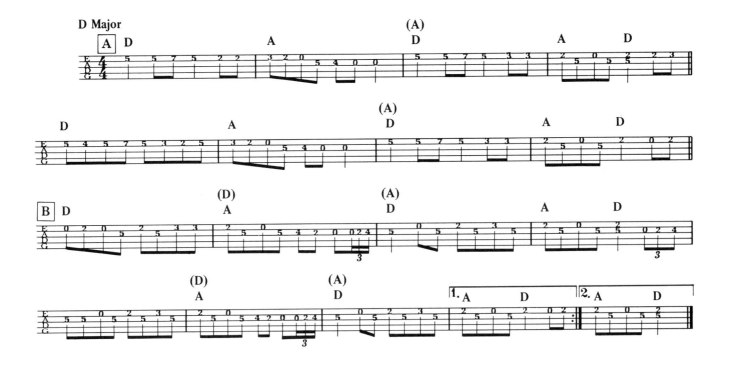

MONEY MUSK A

Reel   Scottish

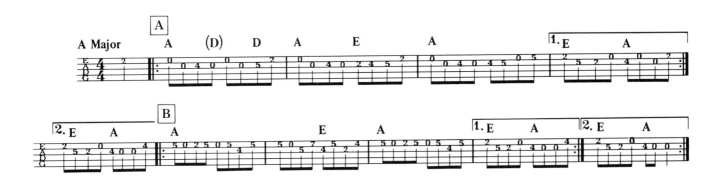

MONEY MUSK B

Old-Time

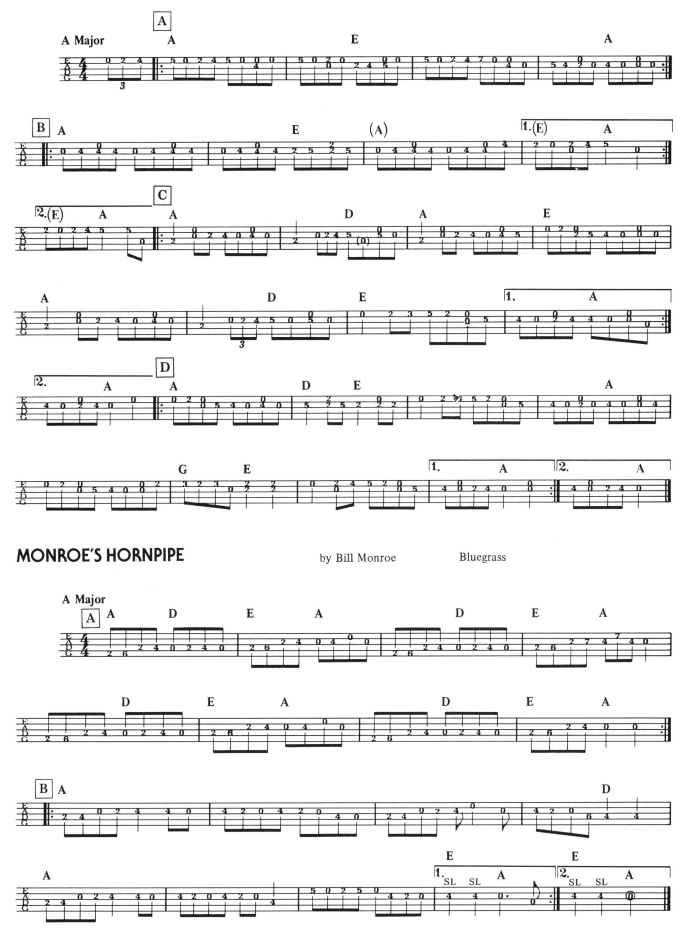

MONROE'S HORNPIPE

by Bill Monroe   Bluegrass

MORGAN MAGAN

by Turlough O'Carolan   Irish

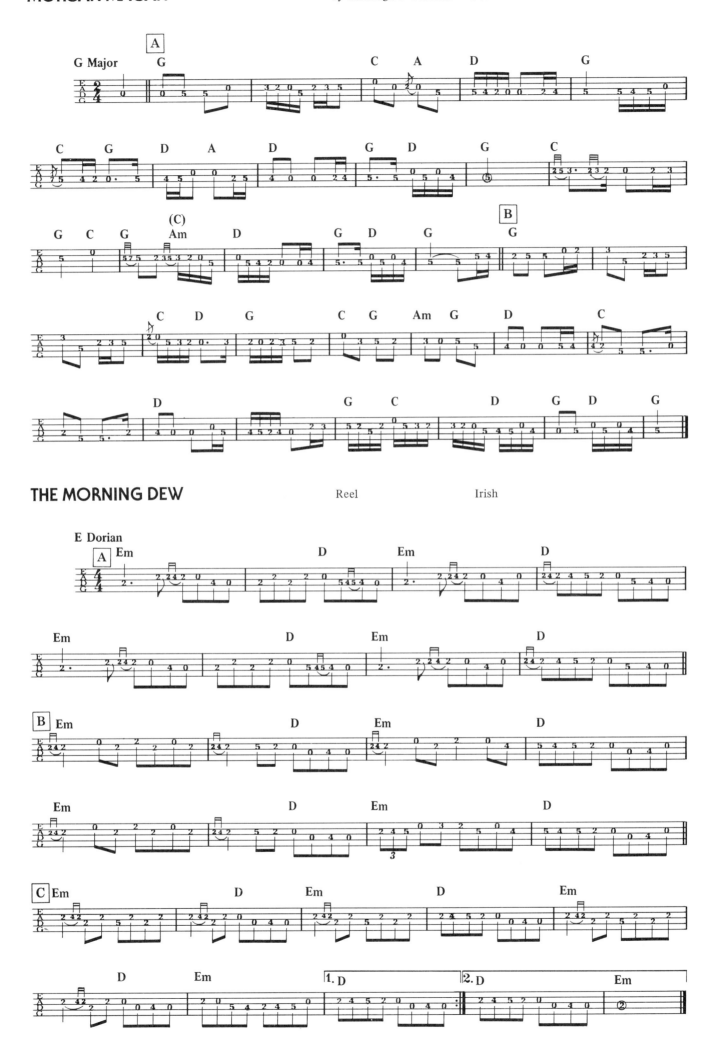

THE MORNING DEW

Reel   Irish

MORPETH RANT

Reel   English
by William Shield

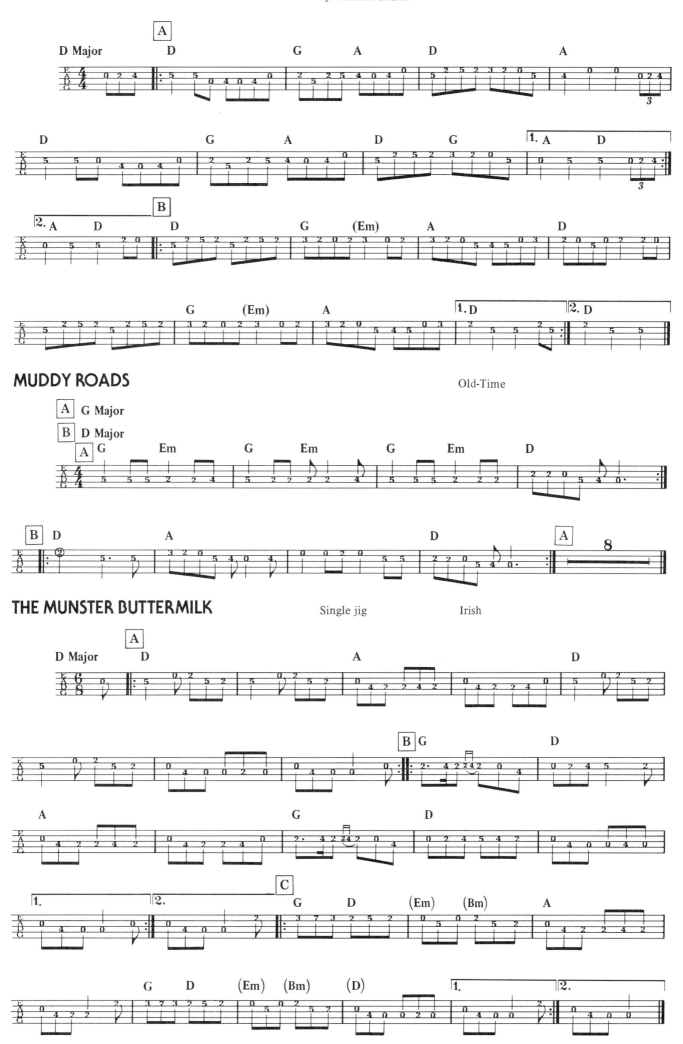

MUDDY ROADS

Old-Time

THE MUNSTER BUTTERMILK

Single jig   Irish

THE MUSICAL PRIEST

Irish

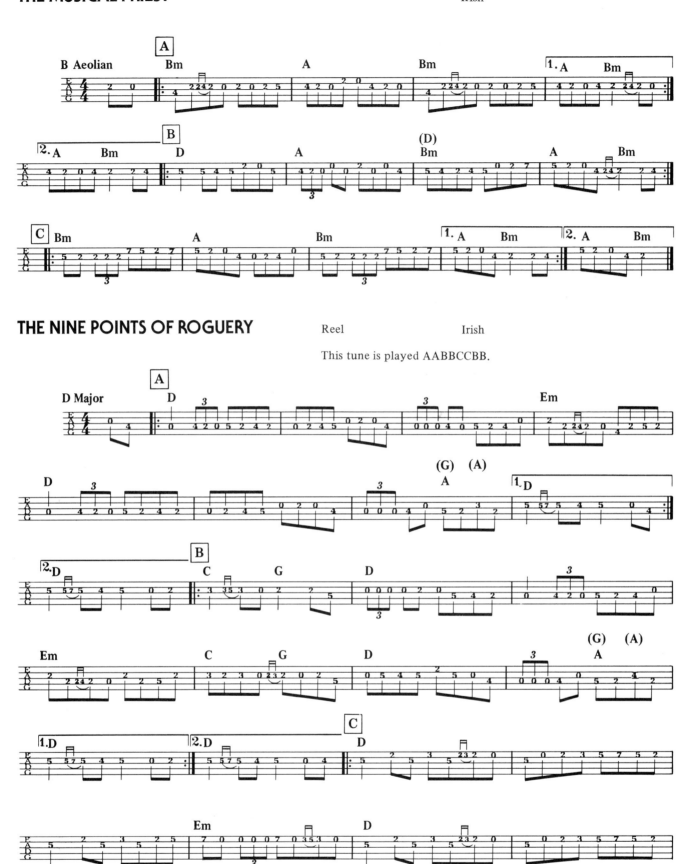

THE NINE POINTS OF ROGUERY

Reel   Irish

This tune is played AABBCCBB.

NONESUCH

English

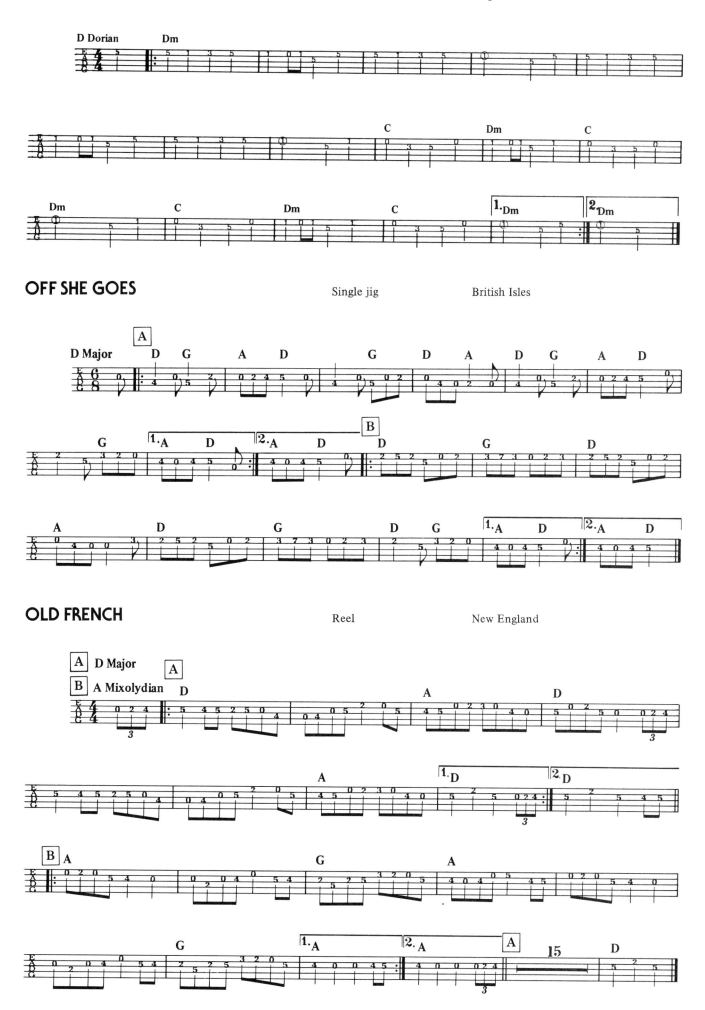

OFF SHE GOES

Single jig   British Isles

OLD FRENCH

Reel   New England

OLD JOE CLARK

Old-Time

In the seventh measure of both the A and B
parts, 5th fret on the D string (G♮) may be
substituted for 6th fret (G♯). If this is done
the accompanying chord will be G Major.

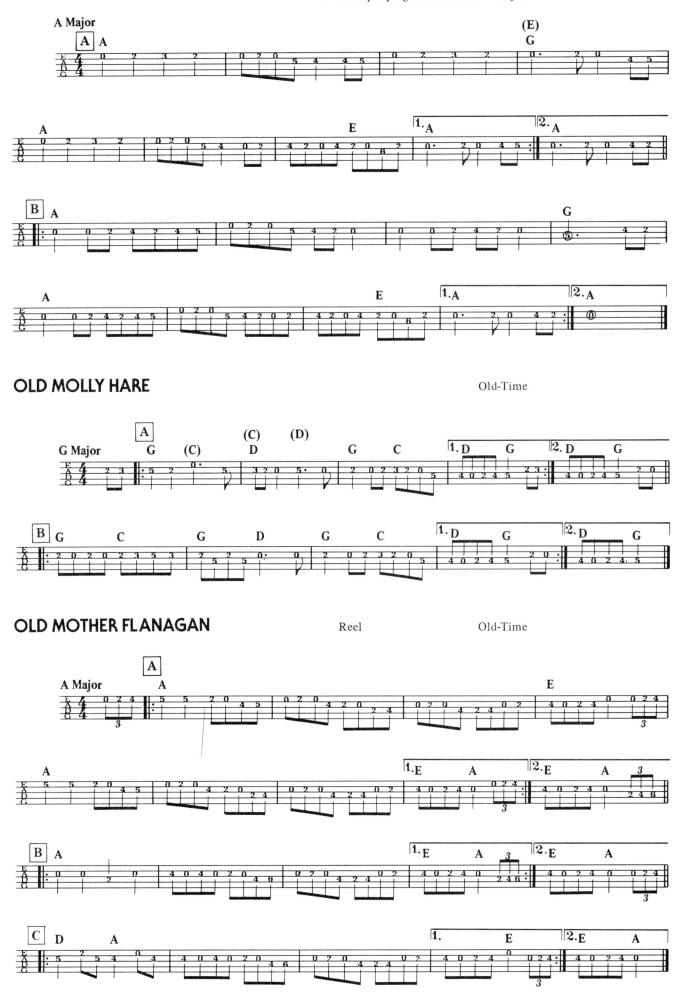

OLD MOLLY HARE

Old-Time

OLD MOTHER FLANAGAN

Reel   Old-Time

OPERA REEL

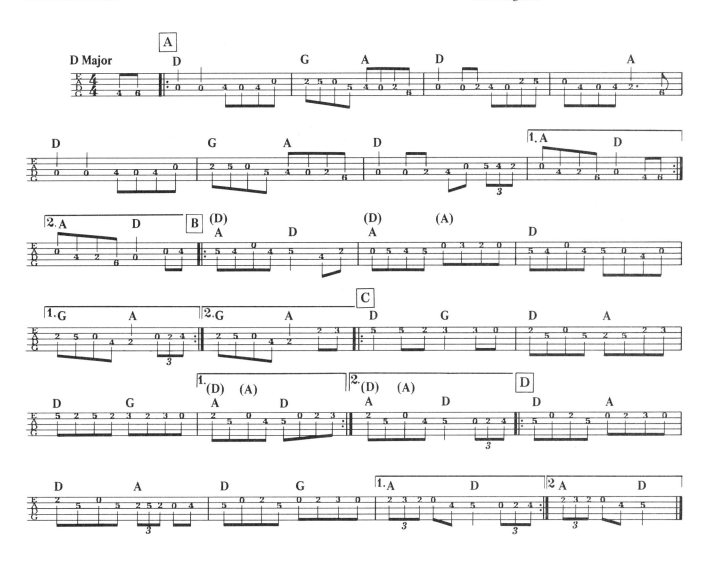

OPUS 57

by David Grisman   Dawg

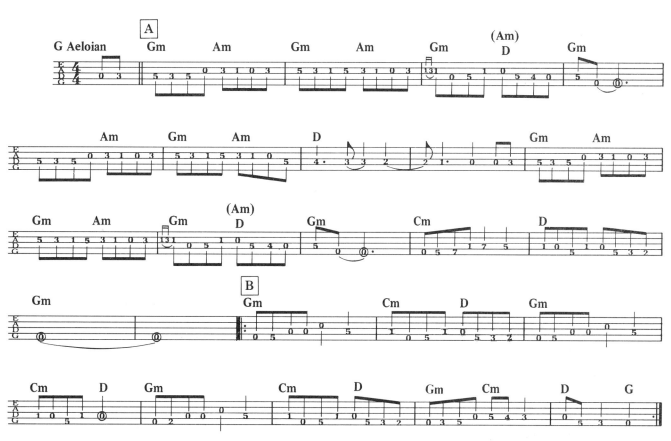

OVER THE WATERFALL

Old-Time

OZARK RAG

Country rag   Old-Time

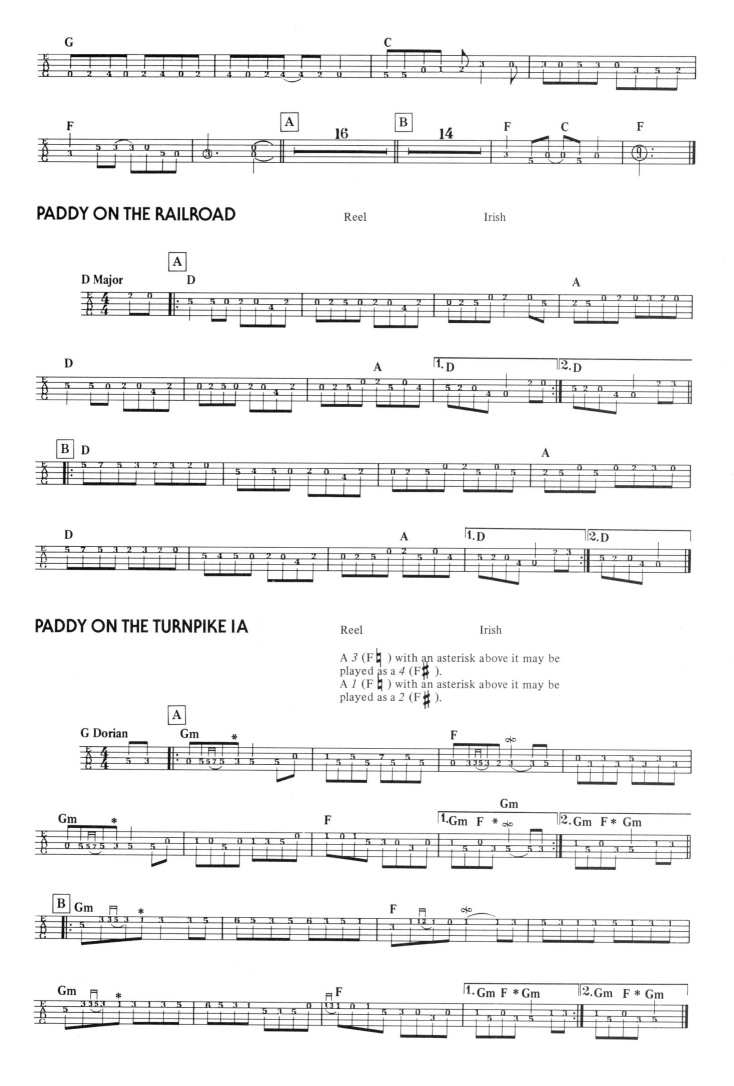

PADDY ON THE RAILROAD

Reel   Irish

PADDY ON THE TURNPIKE IA

Reel   Irish

A *3* (F♮) with an asterisk above it may be
played as a *4* (F♯).
A *1* (F♮) with an asterisk above it may be
played as a *2* (F♯).

PLANXTY DRURY

by Turlough O'Carolan   Irish

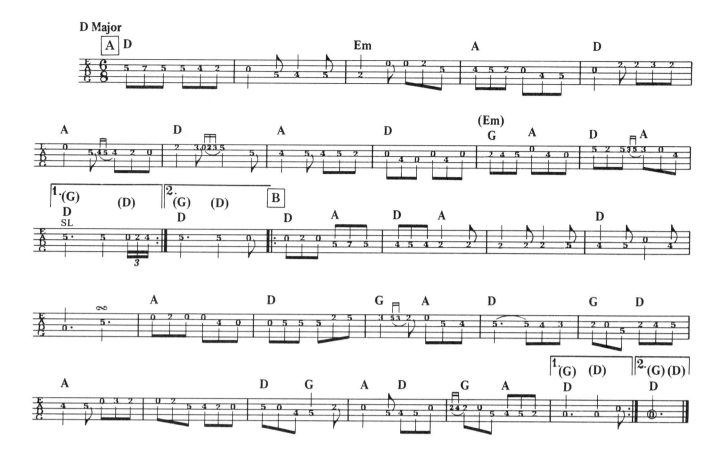

PLANXTY GEORGE BRABAZON

by Turlough O'Carolan   Irish

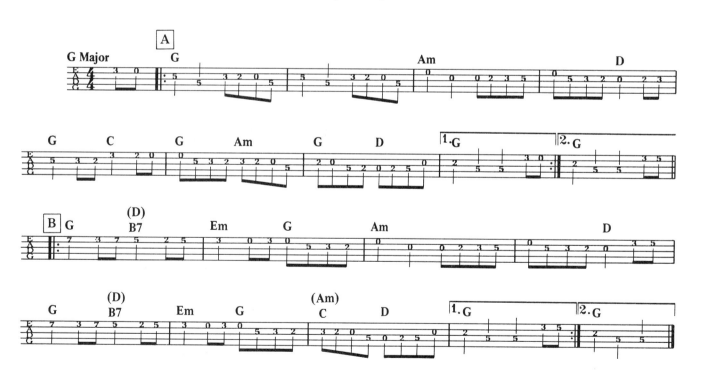

PLANXTY IRWIN

by Turlough O'Carolan   Irish

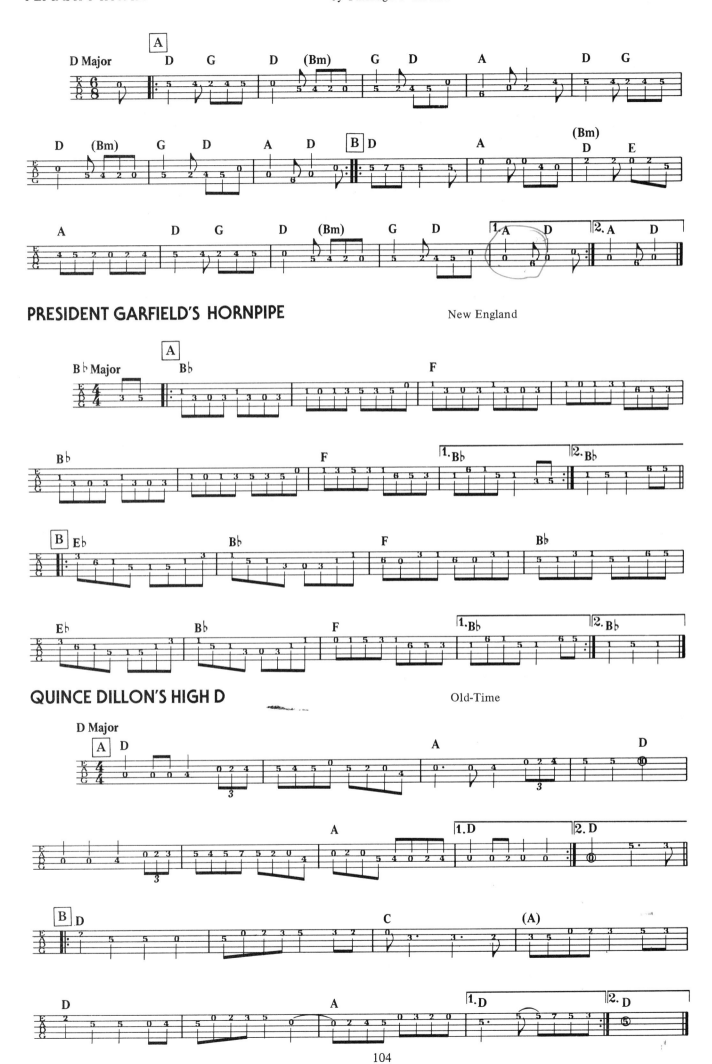

PRESIDENT GARFIELD'S HORNPIPE

New England

QUINCE DILLON'S HIGH D

Old-Time

RAGTIME ANNIE

Old-Time, New
England, Bluegrass

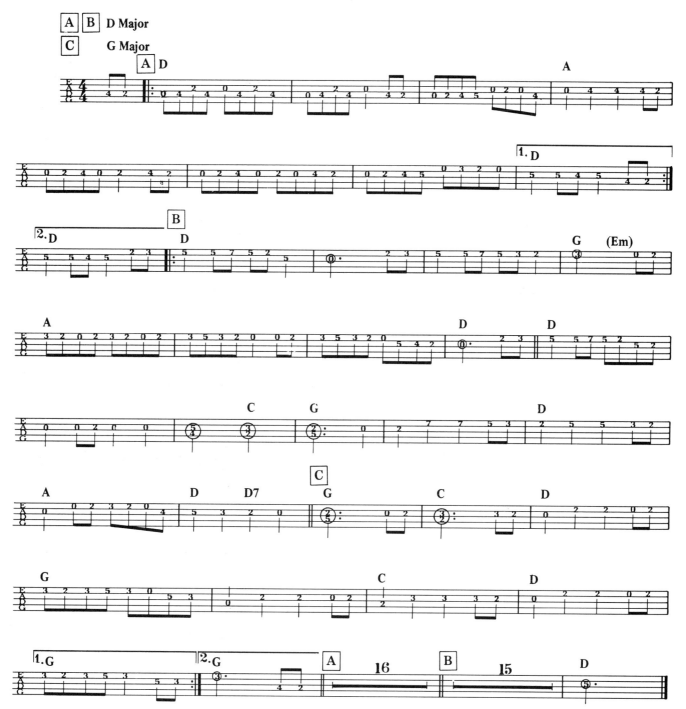

105

RED HAIRED BOY

Reel   Irish

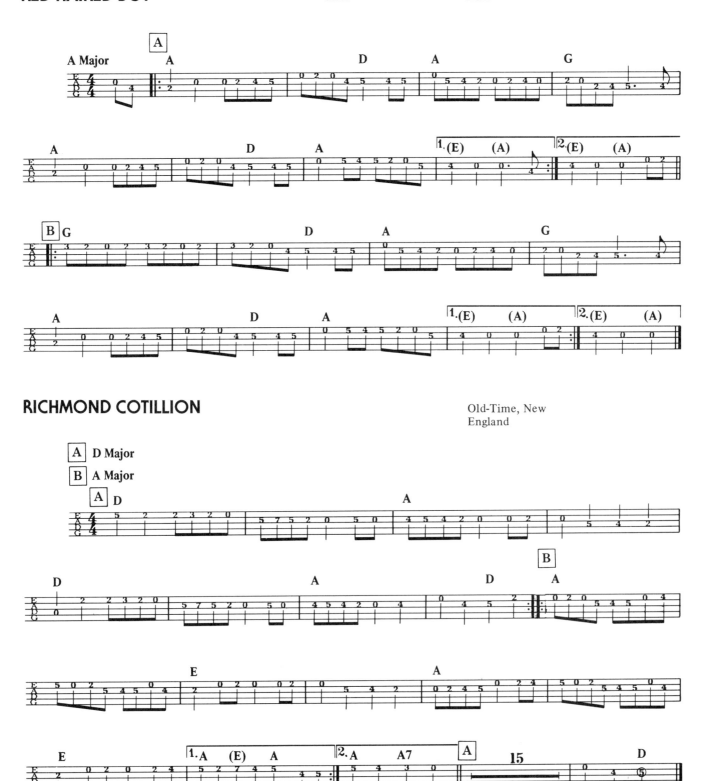

RICHMOND COTILLION

Old-Time, New England

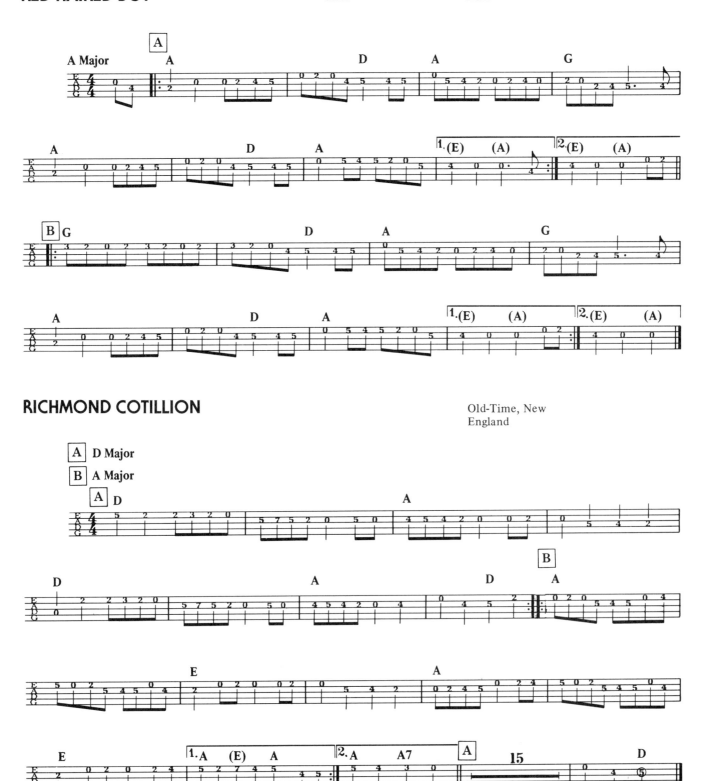

RICKETT'S HORNPIPE

Old-Time, New England

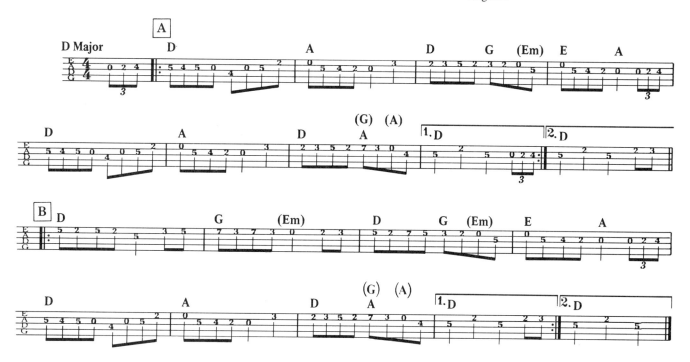

RIGHTS OF MAN

Irish

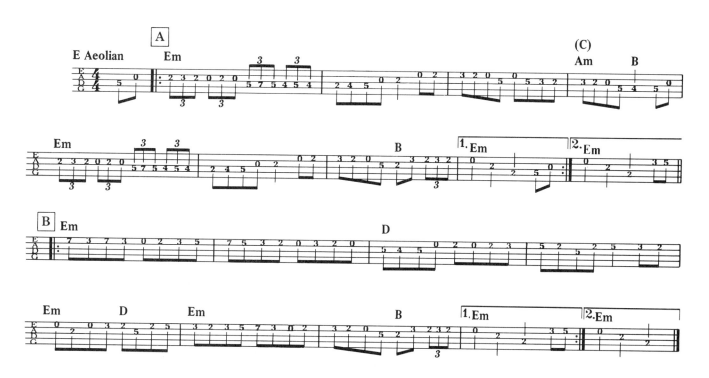

ROCK THE CRADLE JOE

Old-Time

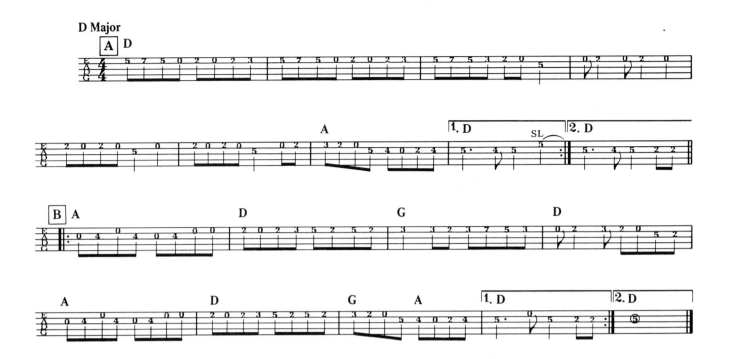

ROCKY MOUNTAIN GOAT

Old-Time

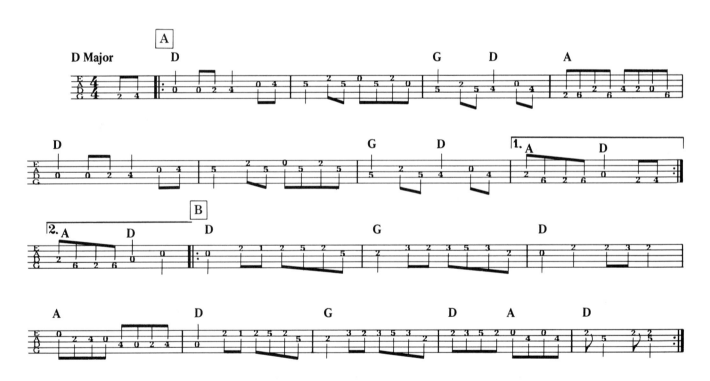

ROCKY ROAD TO DUBLIN I

Slip jig   Irish

A *2* (F♯) with an asterisk above it may be
played as a *1* (F♮).

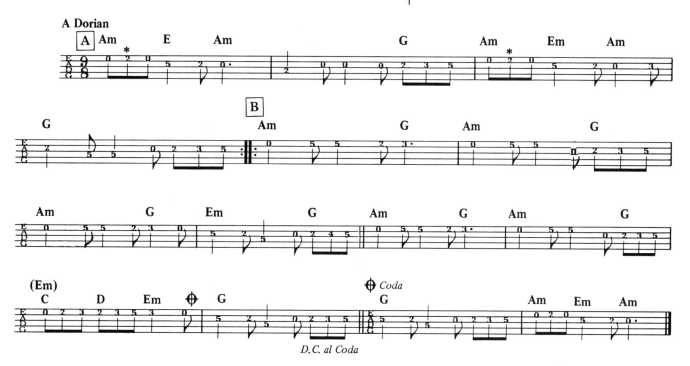

RODNEY'S GLORY

Set dance   Irish

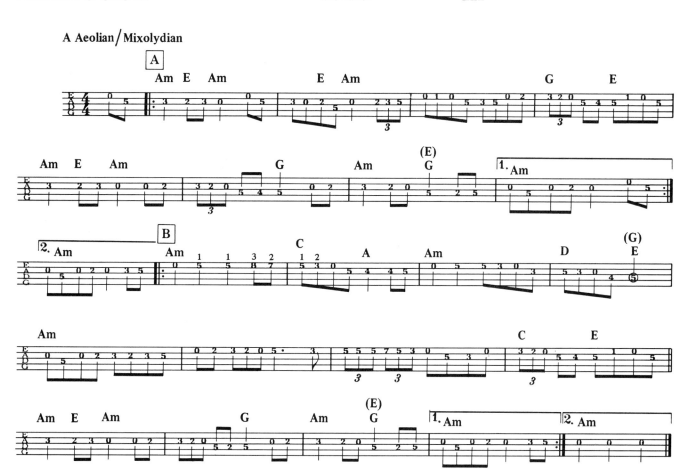

ROSE DIVISION

Old-Time

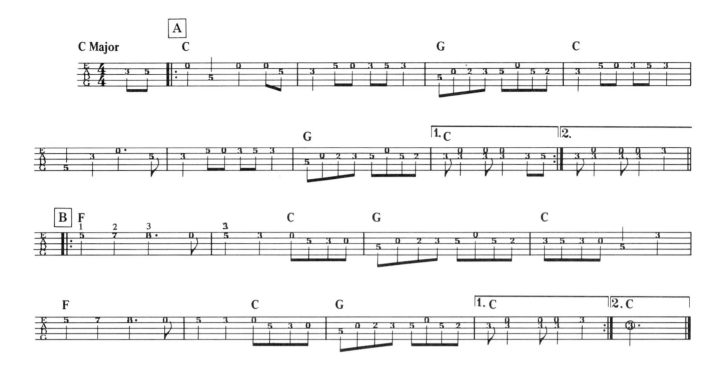

ROSE TREE I

New England

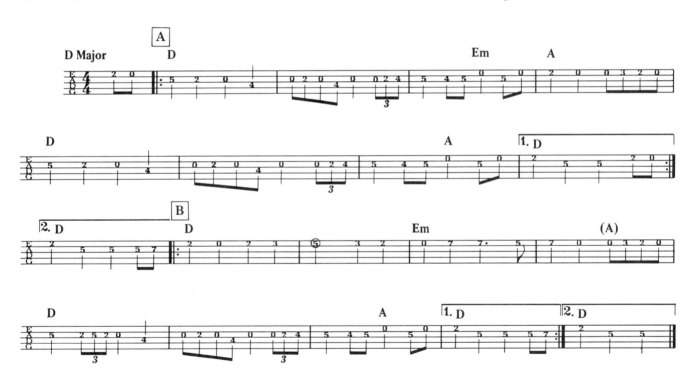

THE ROUTE

Old-Time

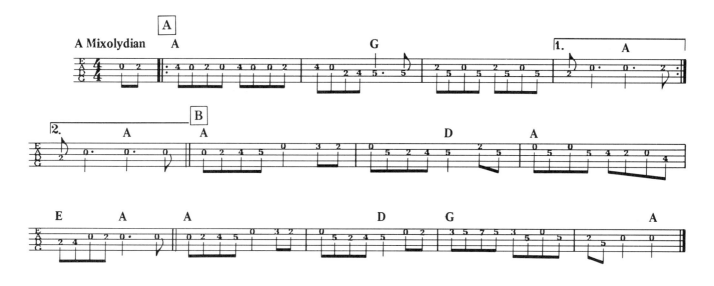

RUN, JOHNNY, RUN A

Bluegrass

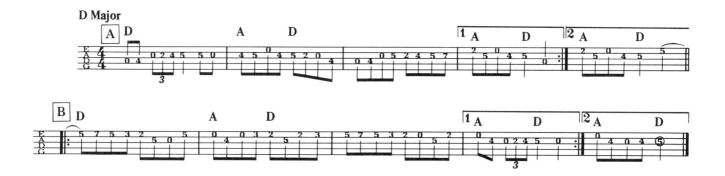

RYE STRAW

Old-Time

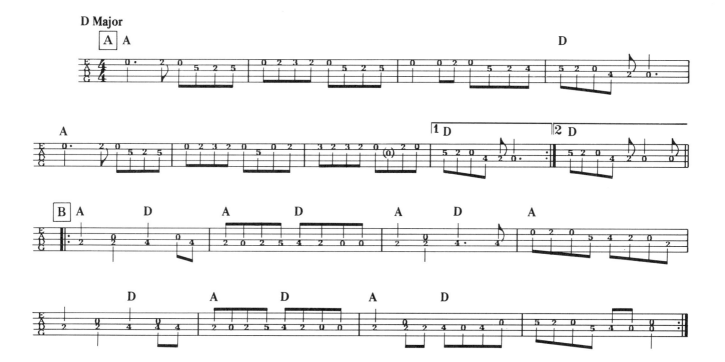

SAIL AWAY LADIES IA

Old-Time

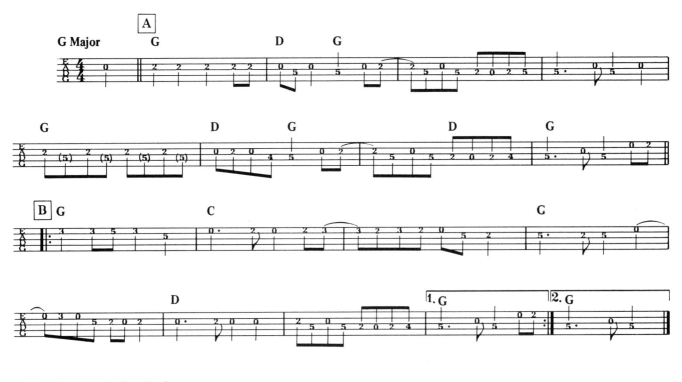

SAIL AWAY LADIES IB

Old-Time, Bluegrass

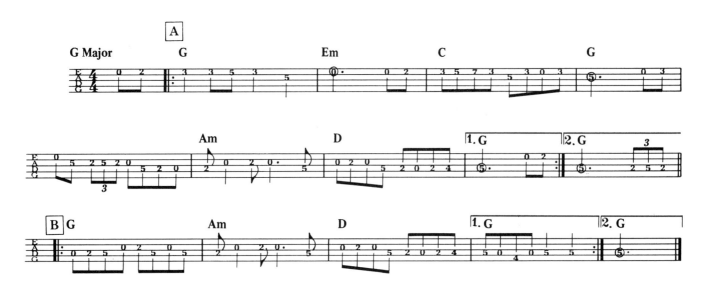

SAIL AWAY LADIES II

Old-Time

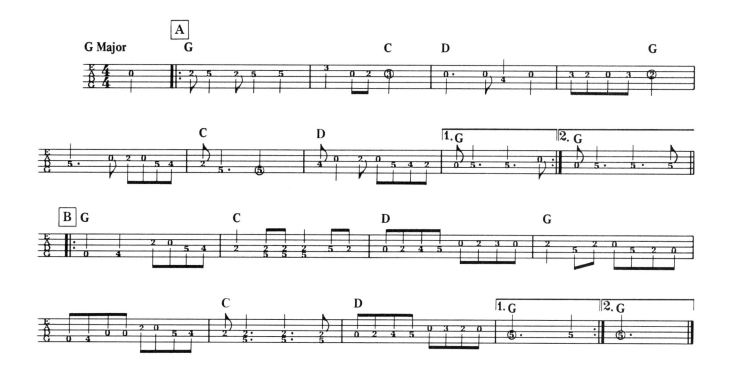

SAILOR'S HORNPIPE

American

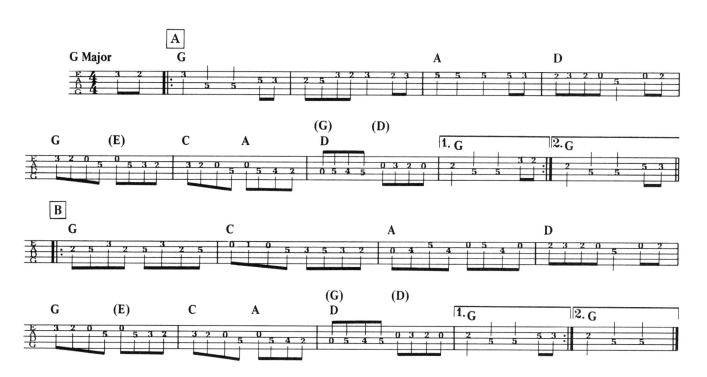

SAINT ANNE'S REEL

Old-Time, New
England

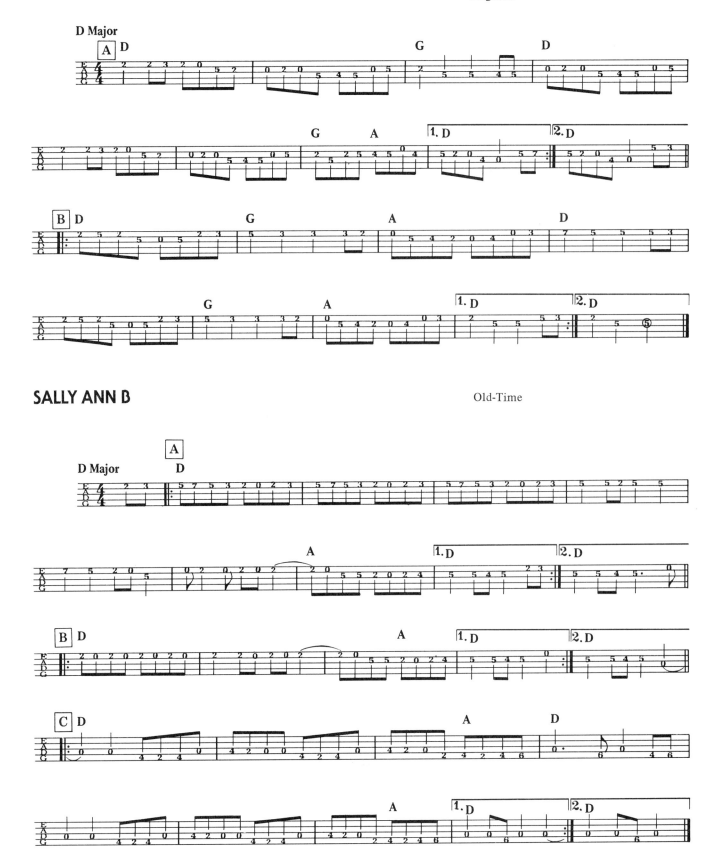

SALLY ANN B

Old-Time

SALLY GOODIN' 2

Old-Time, Bluegrass

SALLY IN THE GARDEN

Old-Time

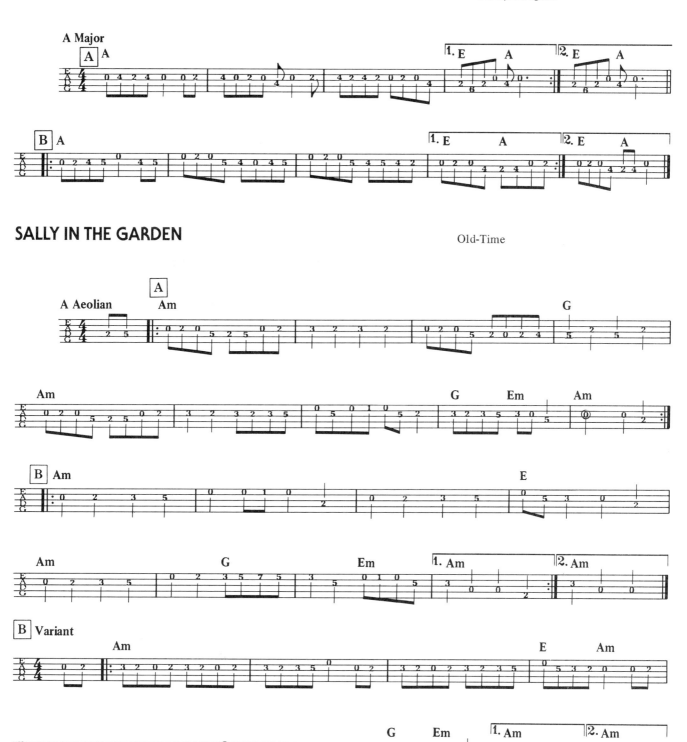

115

SALLY JOHNSON

Old-Time

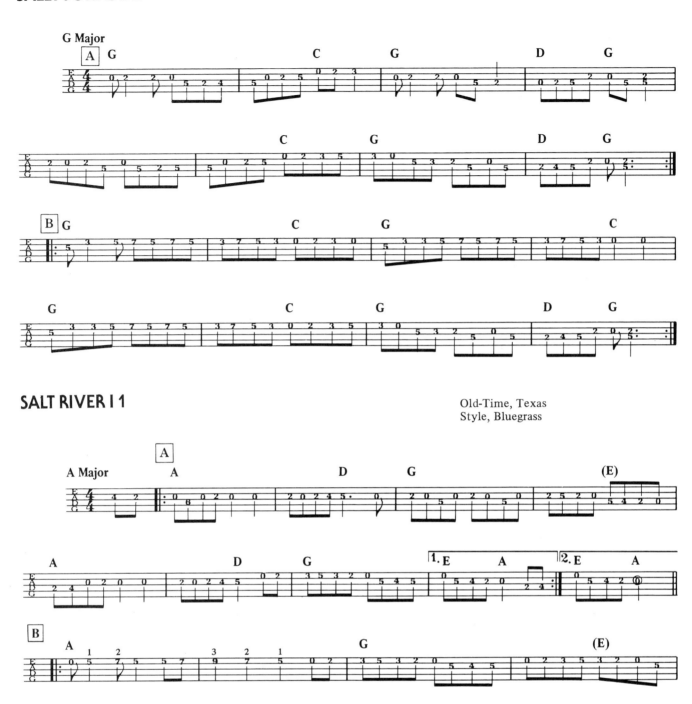

SALT RIVER I 1

Old-Time, Texas
Style, Bluegrass

SANDY RIVER BELLE A 1

Old-Time

D Major

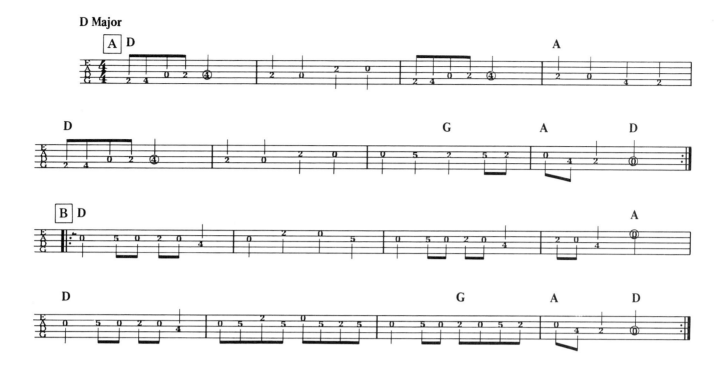

SANTA ANNA'S RETREAT

Old-Time

A Mixolydian

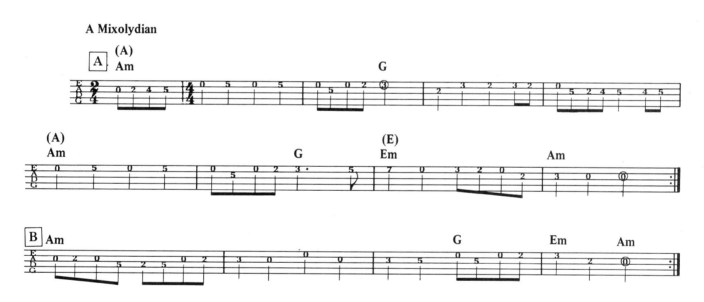

SAY OLD MAN CAN YOU PLAY
THE FIDDLE

Old-Time

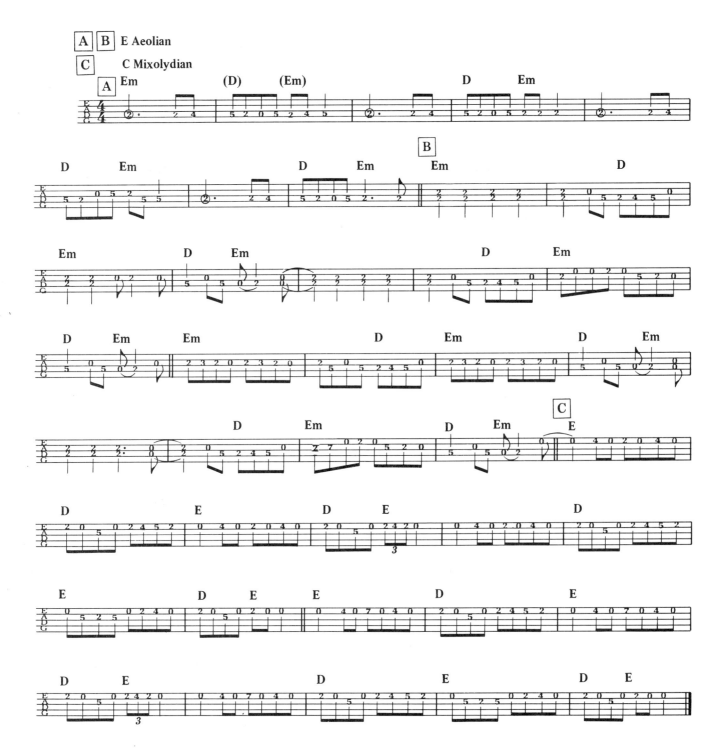

DA SCALLOWAY LASSES

Shetland

SHEEBEG AND SHEEMORE

by Turlough O'Carolan   Irish

SHIP IN THE CLOUDS

Old-Time

SHIPS ARE SAILING

Reel   Irish

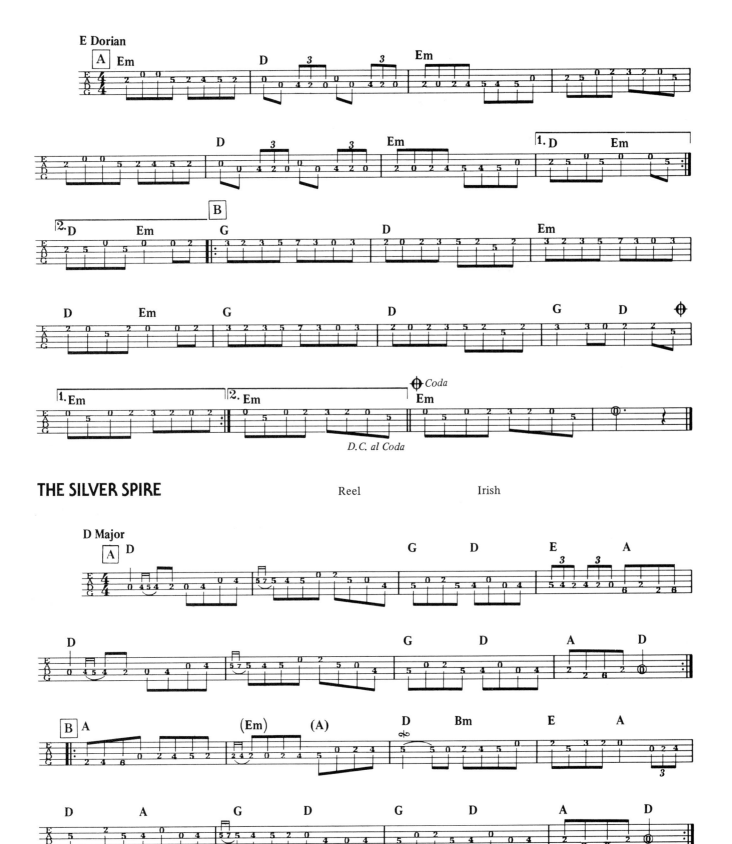

THE SILVER SPIRE

Reel   Irish

SLEEP SOOND IDA MOARNIN'

Reel   Shetland

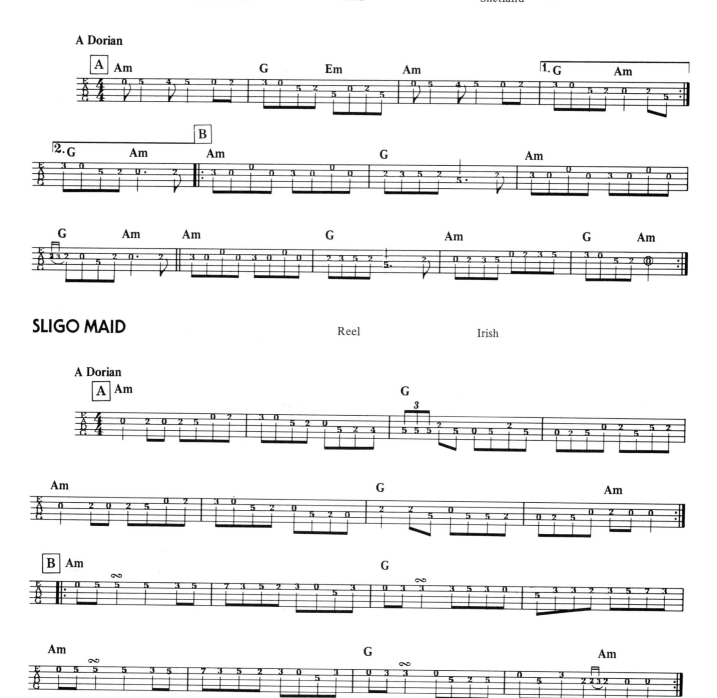

SLIGO MAID

Reel   Irish

SMITH'S REEL

Texas Style, Western Swing

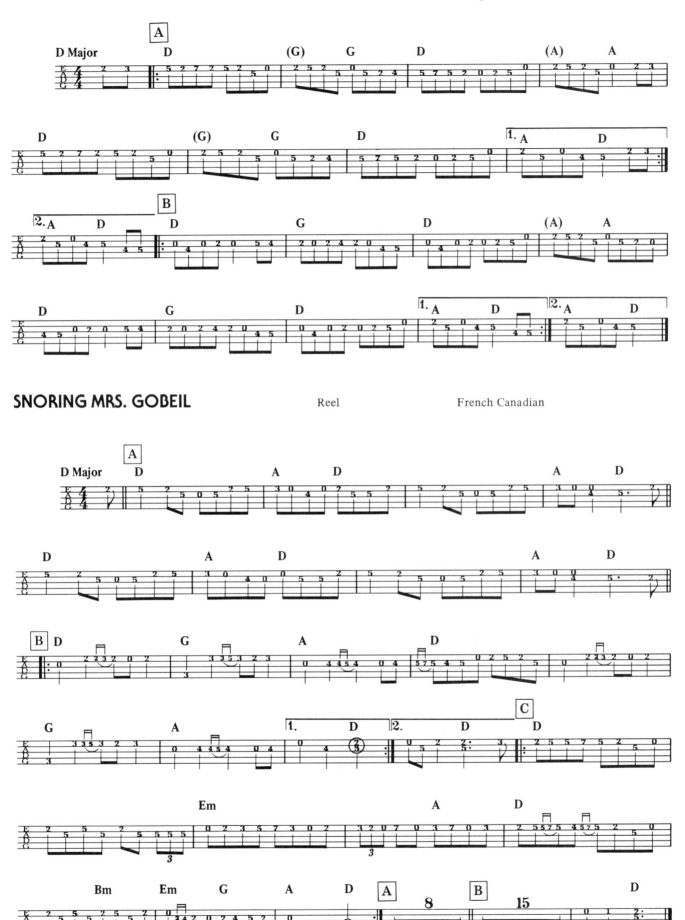

SNORING MRS. GOBEIL

Reel   French Canadian

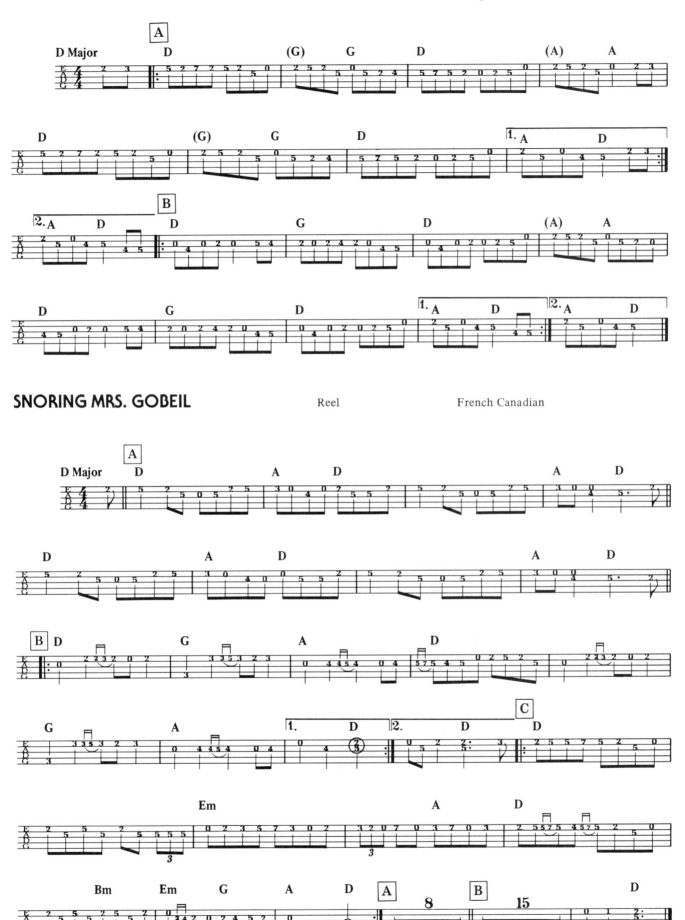

SNOWFLAKE REEL

Bluegrass

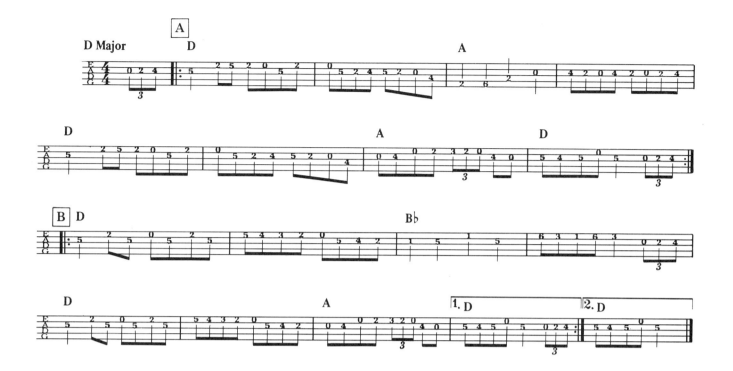

SNOWSHOES A

Old-Time, Bluegrass

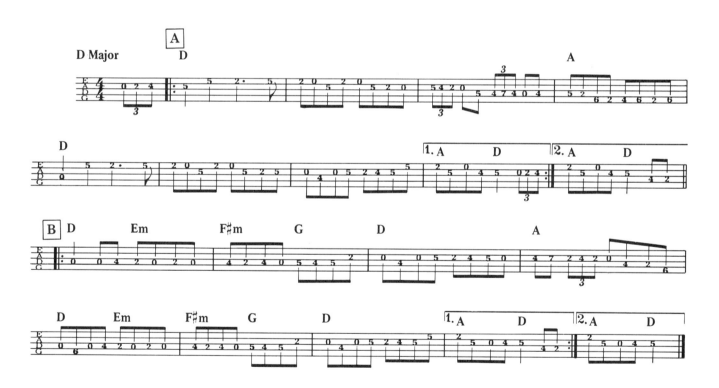

SOLDIER'S JOY

Old-Time, Bluegrass

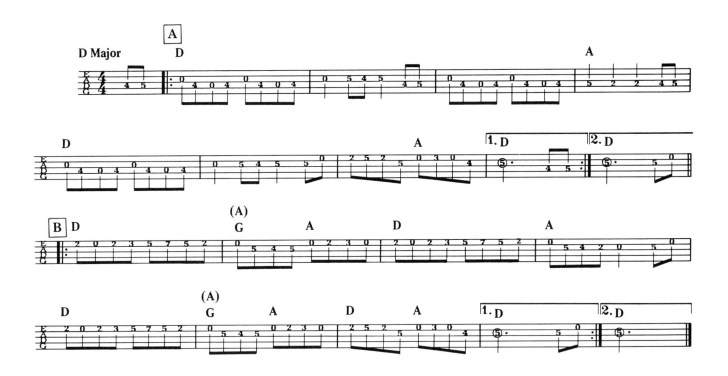

SONNY'S MAZURKA

Irish

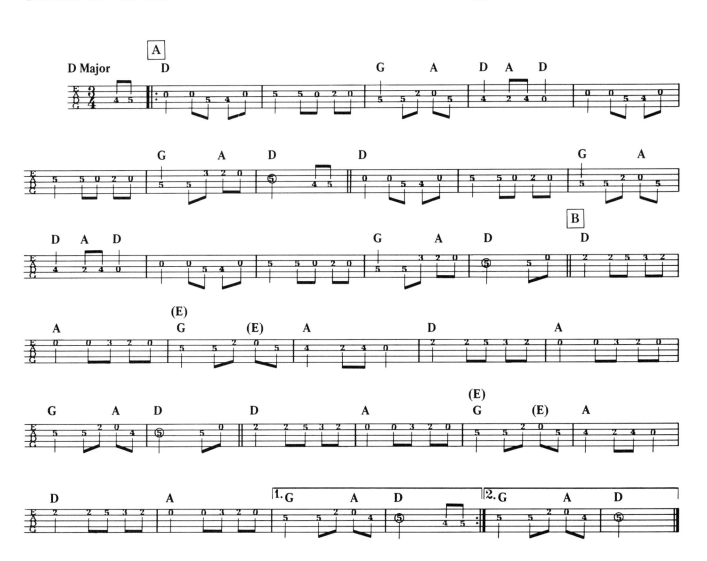

SOUTHWIND

Irish

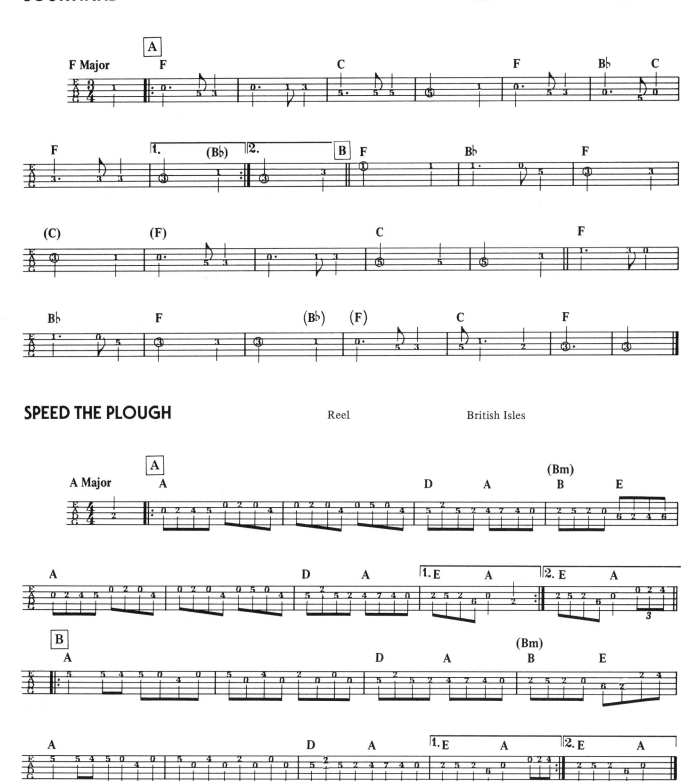

SPEED THE PLOUGH

Reel

British Isles

THE STAR ABOVE THE GARTER

Single jig   Irish

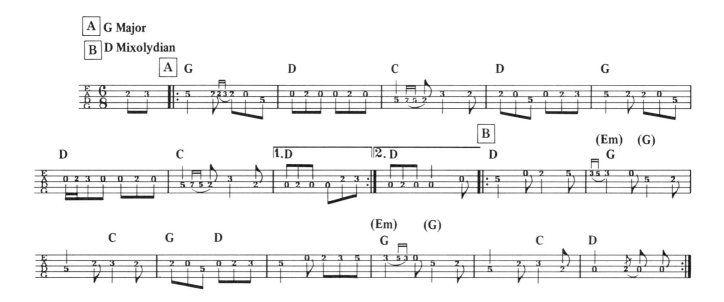

THE STAR OF MUNSTER

Reel   Irish

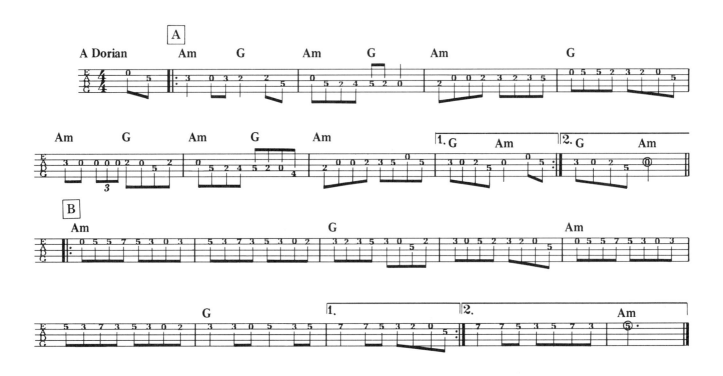

STAR OF THE COUNTY DOWN

Irish

STATEN ISLAND

Hornpipe, Reel   Old-Time, New England

STONE'S RAG

Country rag

Old-Time, Texas
Style

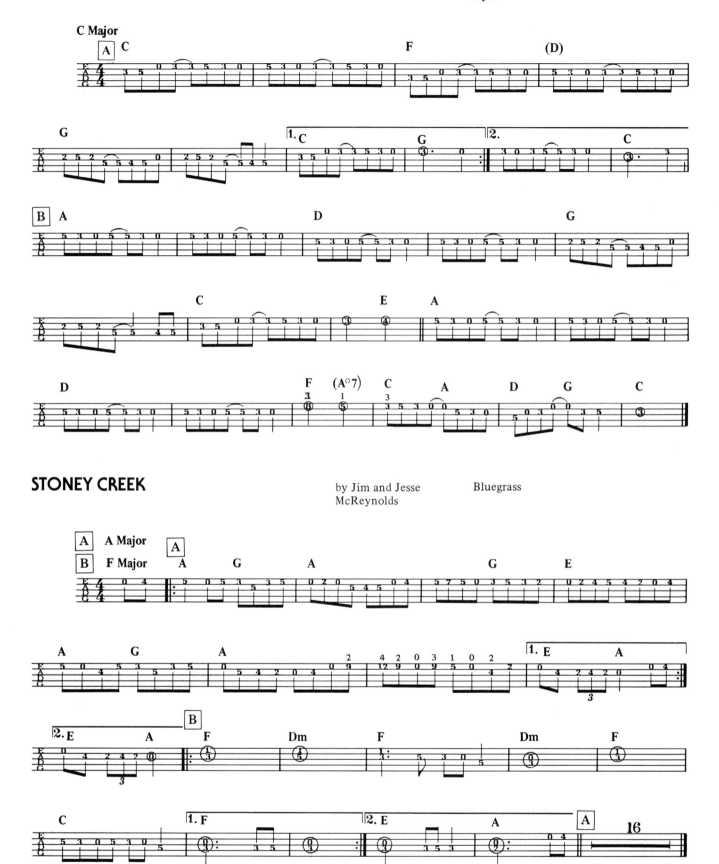

STONEY CREEK

by Jim and Jesse
McReynolds

Bluegrass

STONEY POINT

British Isles,
American

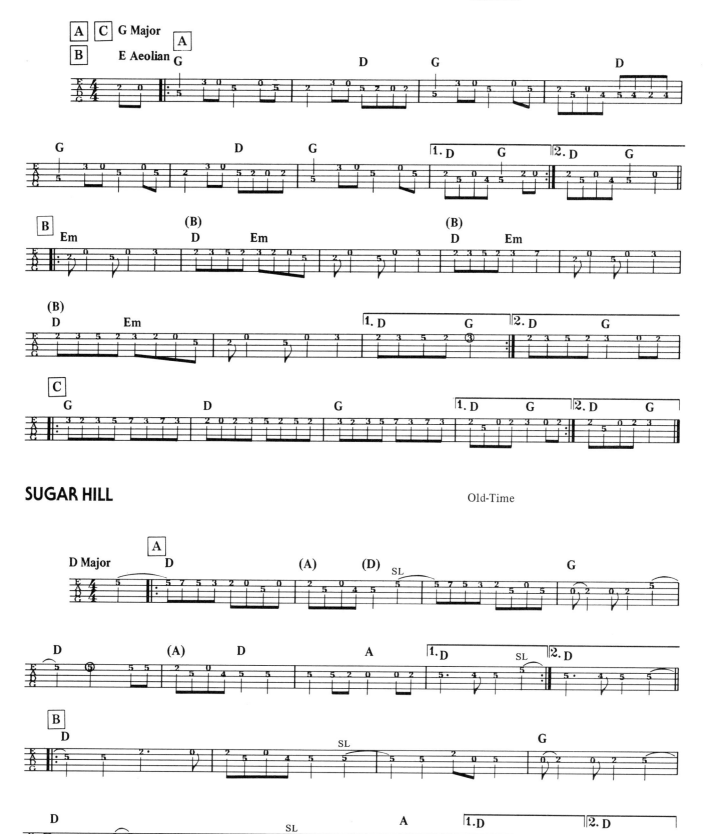

SUGAR HILL

Old-Time

SUGAR IN THE GOURD

Old-Time

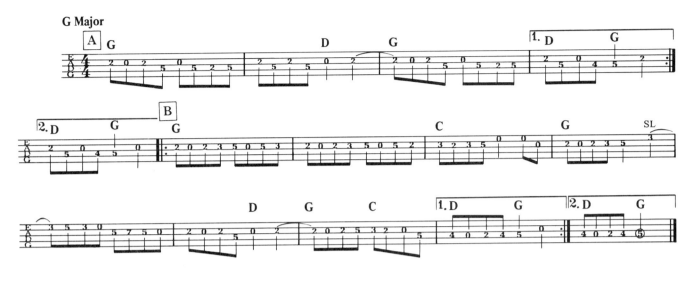

THE SWALLOW'S TAIL REEL

Irish

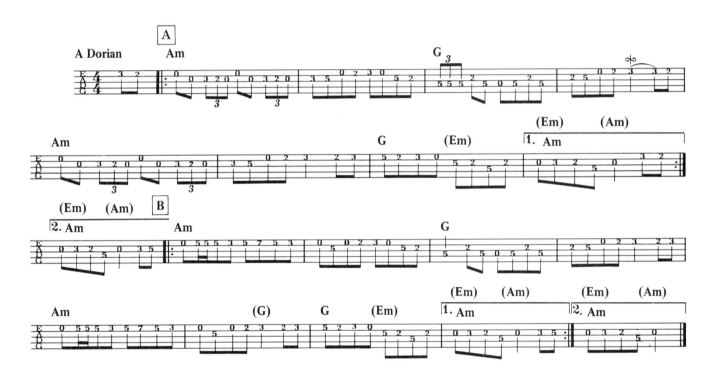

THE SWALLOW TAIL JIG

Double jig   Irish

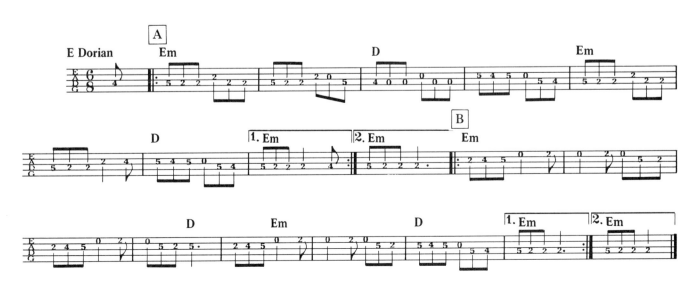

SWINGING ON A GATE

British Isles, New England

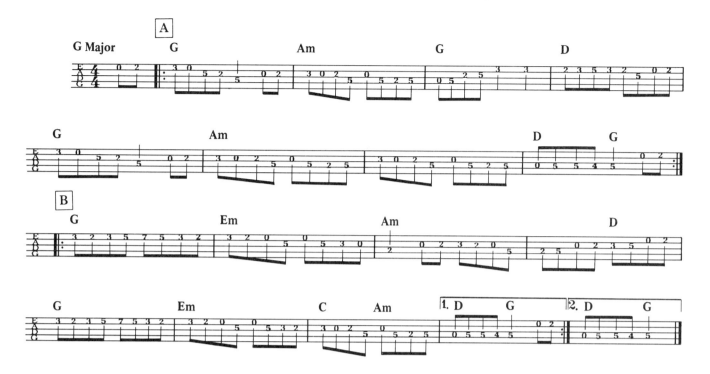

TAKE ME BACK TO GEORGIA

Old-Time

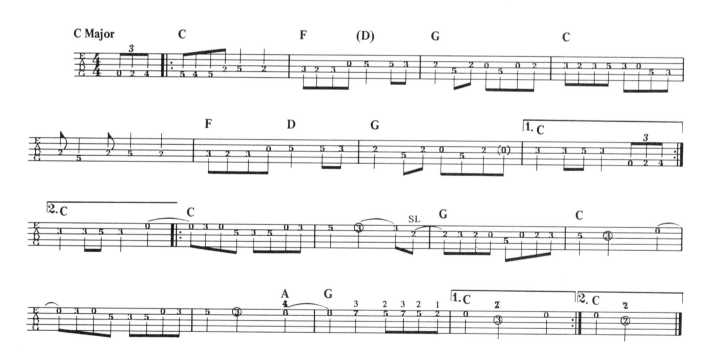

TARBOLTON REEL

Irish, French
Canadian

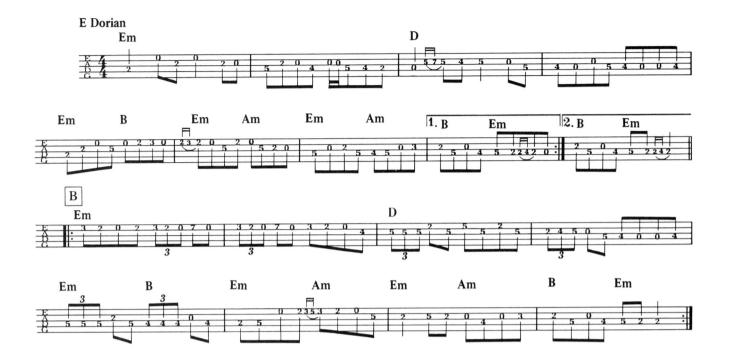

TEMPERANCE REEL

Irish

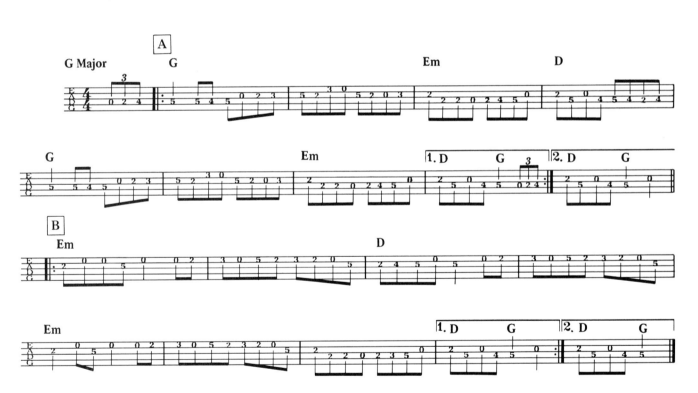

TEXAS GALES

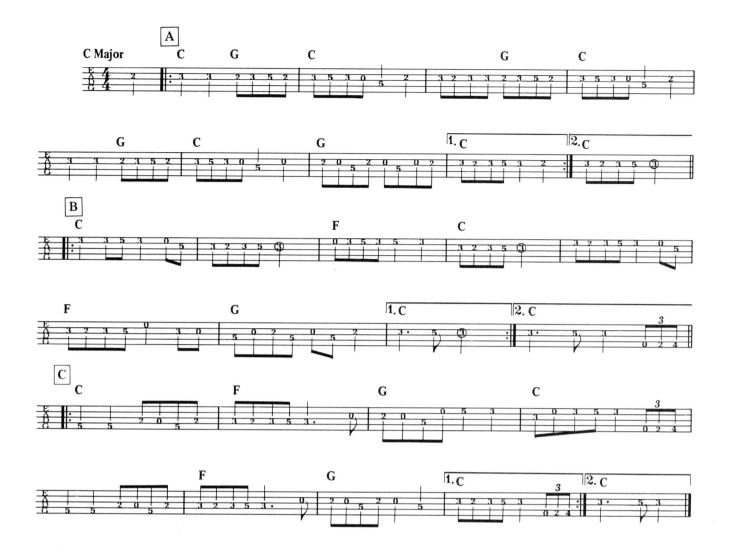

THERE'S A BROWN SKIN GAL

Old-Time

THREE-IN-ONE TWO-STEP

Country rag   Old-Time

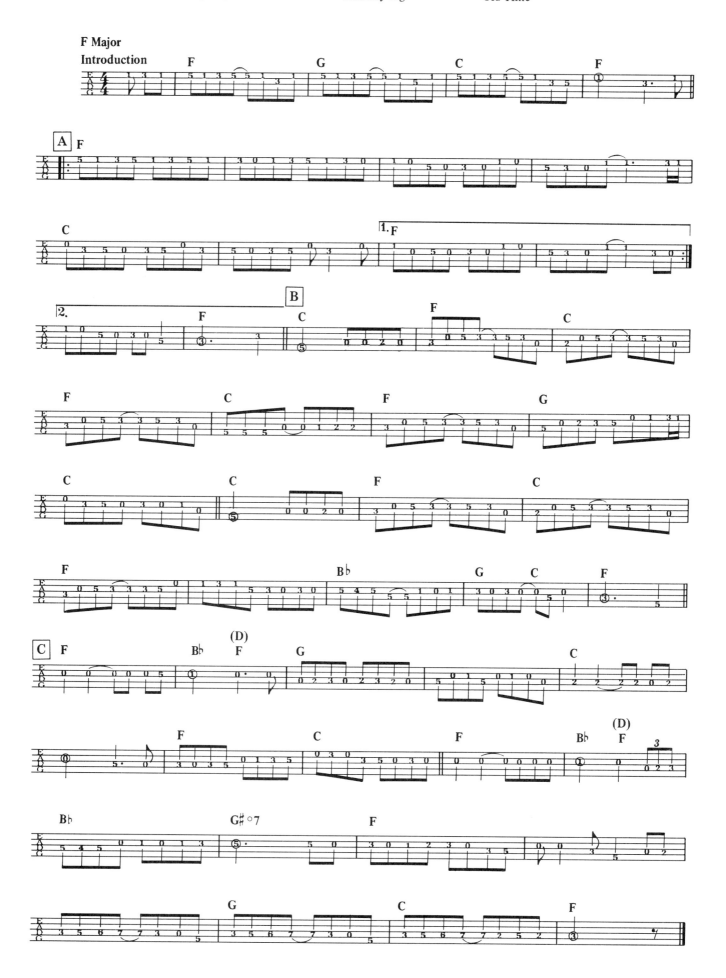

TIMOUR THE TARTAR

Reel   British Isles

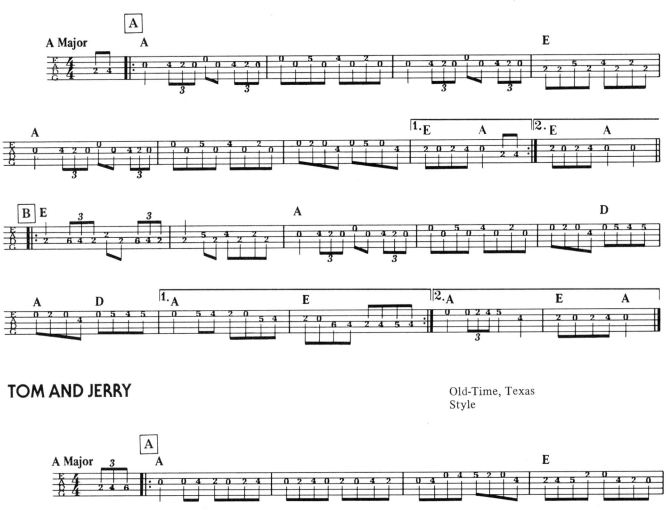

TOM AND JERRY

Old-Time, Texas
Style

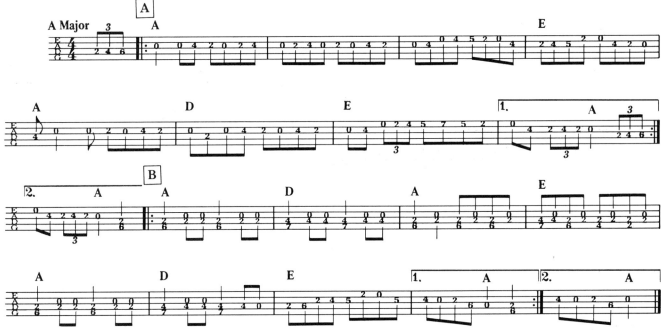

136

TOO YOUNG TO MARRY

British Isles,
American

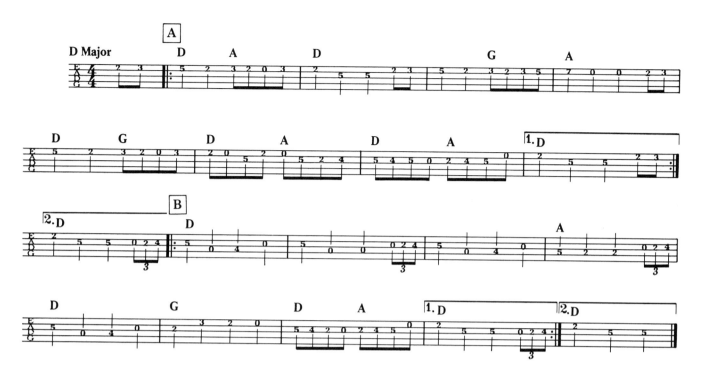

TURKEY IN THE STRAW

Old-Time, Bluegrass

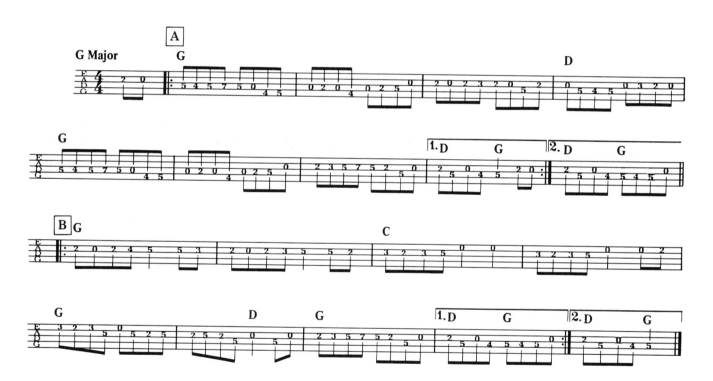

TWINKLE LITTLE STAR

Old-Time, Texas
Style

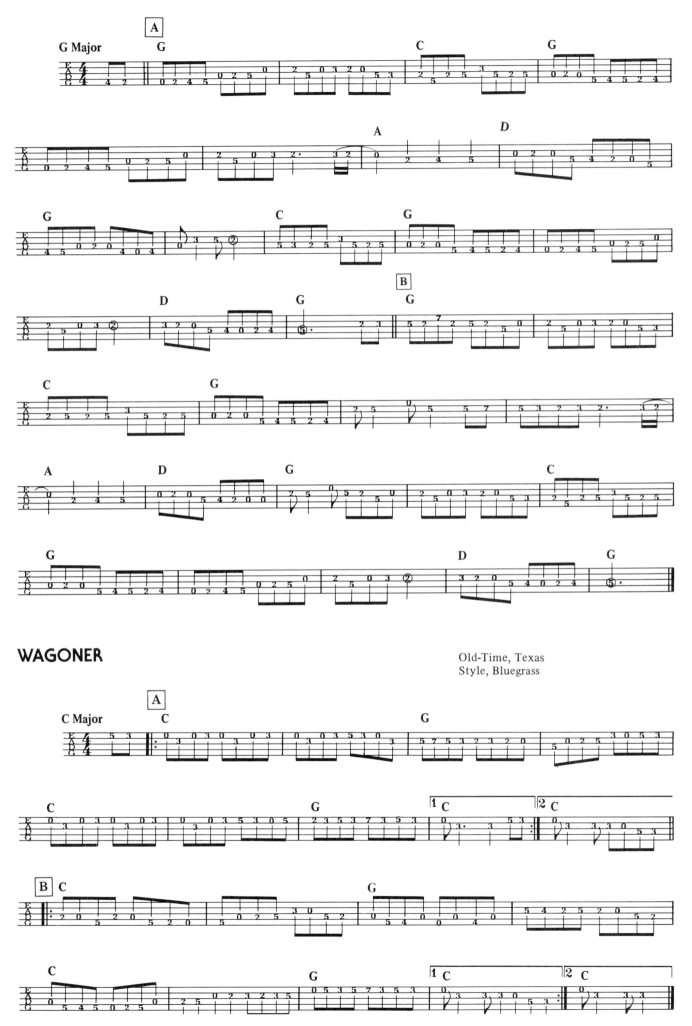

WAGONER

Old-Time, Texas
Style, Bluegrass

WAKE UP SUSAN I

Old-Time

A version of this tune uses the A part of "Miller's Reel" as a B part. If this is done, the B and C parts in the written version are not used.

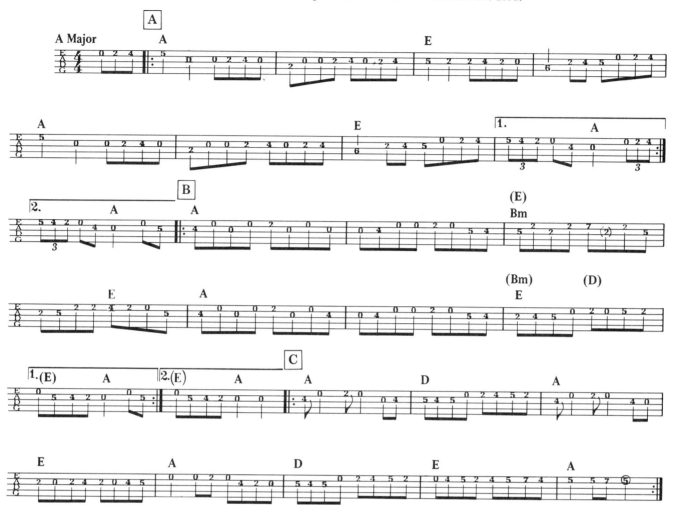

WALKING IN MY SLEEP

Old-Time, Bluegrass

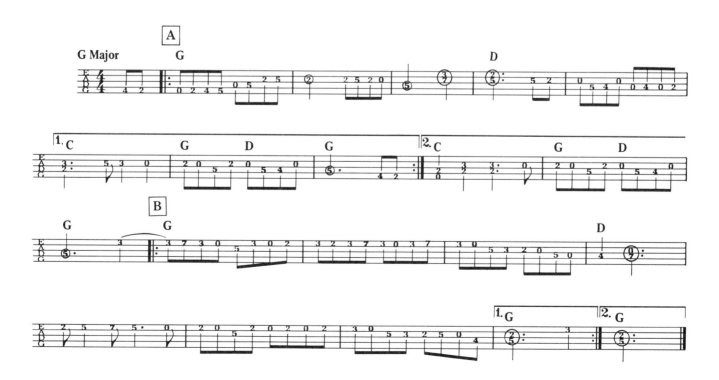

WESTERN COUNTRY

Old-Time

WEST FORK GALS

Old-Time

THE WHEELS OF THE WORLD

Reel   Irish

A *3* (C♮) with an asterisk above it may be
played as a *4* (C♯).

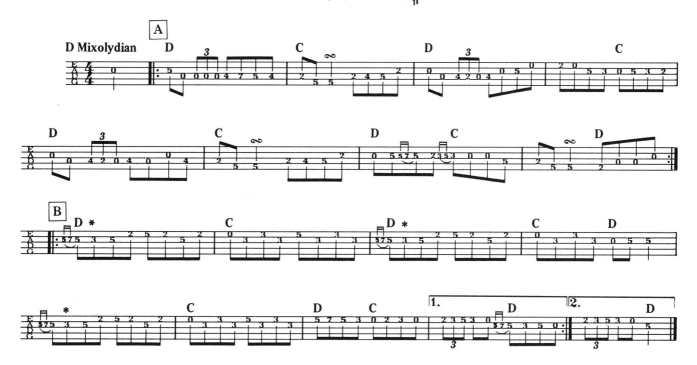

WHISKEY BEFORE BREAKFAST

Old-Time

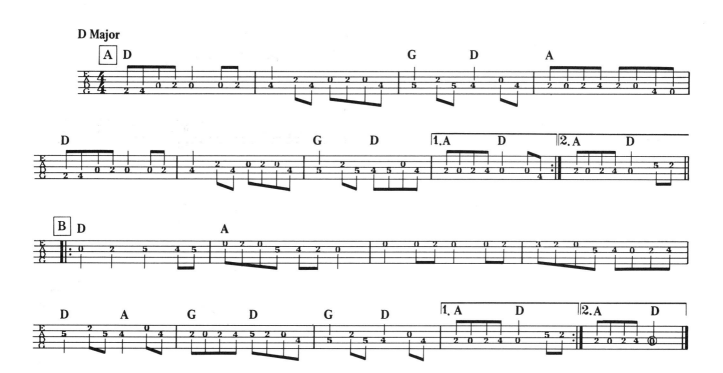

141

THE WHITE COCKADE

Reel   British Isles

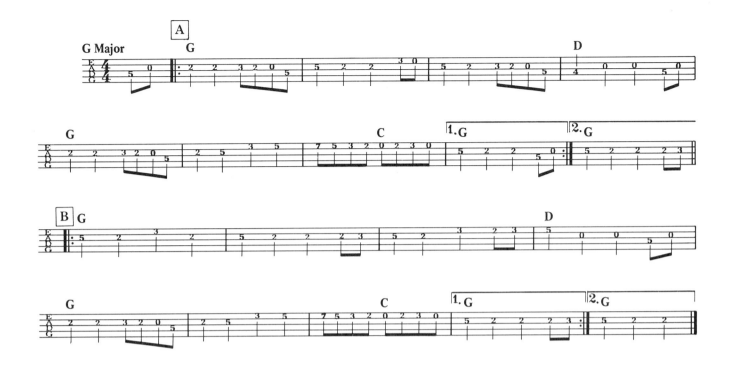

WHITE HORSE BREAKDOWN

by Bill Monroe   Bluegrass

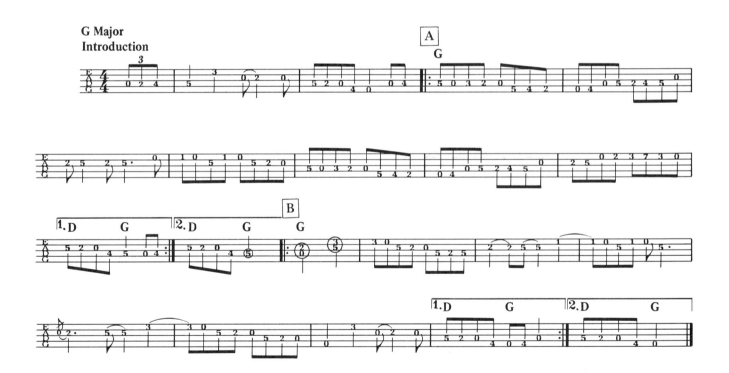

THE WIND THAT SHAKES THE BARLEY

Reel   Irish

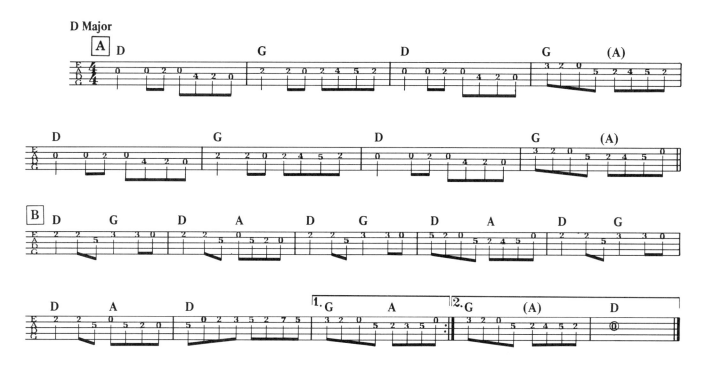

THE WISE MAID

Reel   Irish

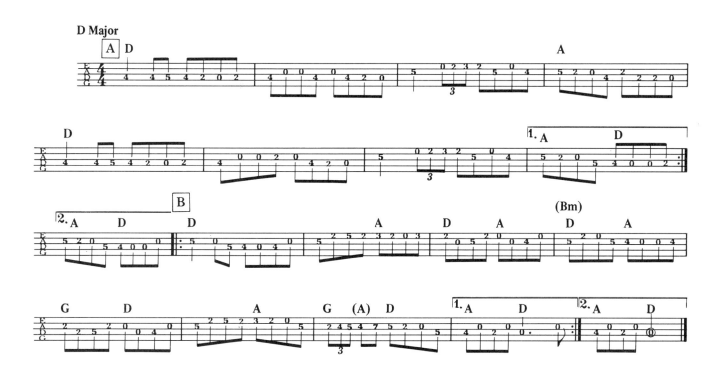

DISCOGRAPHY

A General Discography Indexed by Tune Title

The Format:

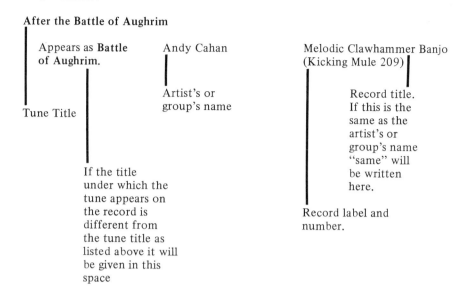

An asterisk to the left of the artist's or group's name indicates that I have relied more on their recording of the tune than on others. Listening to this recording in each case will serve to bulwark the foundations of rhythm and melody and elucidate the fineries of ornament and stylistic nuance. The written music is only half the story, and if unequal halves are a possibility, it is the lesser of the two.

Titles in parentheses (see "Blackberry Blossom") are not included in the tune section of this book. These titles and their sources are listed below in hopes that different pieces of the same name will not be confused.

After the Battle of Aughrim

Appears as **Battle of Aughrim**.

Andy Cahan	Melodic Clawhammer Banjo (Kicking Mule 209)

Appears as part of the medley **Battle of Aughrim**.

*Chieftains	Chieftains 4 (Claddagh 14)

Appears as **Battle of Aughrim**.

Jody Stecher	Snake Baked a Hoecake (Bay 203)

Angeline the Baker

Kenny Hall and the Sweets Mill String Band	Same (Bay 727)
Pickin' around the Cookstove	Same (Rounder 0040)
Roaring Fork Ramblers	Galax 73 (Tennvale 002)
Wretched Refuse	Same (Beet 7003)

Angus Campbell

Leo Beaudoin	Old Time Fiddler's Contest 7/30/77 (Green Mountain 1026)
Jana Greif	I Love Fiddlin' (American Heritage 516)
Sonja Nordstrom	Old Time Fiddler's Contest 7/26/75 (Green Mountain 1050)
?	25 Old Tyme Fiddle Hits (K-Tel FH1)
Jay Ungar and Lyn Hardy	Catskill Mountain Goosechase (Philo 1040)
Yankee Ingenuity	Kitchen Junket (Fretless 200A)

Another Jig Will Do

Boys of the Lough	Live (Philo 1026)

Arkansas Traveler

*Kenny Baker	Farmyard Swing (County 775)
Byron Berline	Dad's Favorites (Rounder 0100)
Byron Berline	Fiddle Jam Session (Voyager 301)
Curly Ray Cline	My Little Home in West Virginia (Rebel 1515)

Cockerham, Jarrell, and Jenkins	Back Home in the Blue Ridge (County 723)
Jana Greif	I Love Fiddlin' (American Heritage 516)
Earl Johnson and His Clodhoppers	Hell Broke Loose in Georgia (County 514)
Clark Kessinger	Live at Union Grove (Folkways FA 2337)
Bill Long and Bill Mitchell	More Fiddle Jam Sessions (Voyager 304)
Pete Parish	Clawhammer Banjo (Tennvale 003)
Eck Robertson and Henry Gilliland	Master Fiddler (Sonyatone 201)
Eck Robertson and Henry Gilliland	Texas Farewell (County 517)
Art Rosenbaum	The Art of the Mountain Banjo (Kicking Mule 203)
Buck Ryan	Draggin' the Bow (Rebel 1552)
Blaine Sprouse	Same (Rounder 0117)
Roger Sprung	Ragtime Bluegrass 2 (Folkways FA 2371)
?	25 Old Tyme Fiddle Hits (K-Tel FH1)
Gene White Jr.	Old Time Fiddler's Contest 7/26/75 (Green Mountain 1050)

Athole Highlanders, The

Boys of the Lough	Piper's Broken Finger (Philo 1042)
*Dave Swarbrick	Swarbrick 2 (Transatlantic 341)

Avalon Quickstep

*Arm and Hammer String Band	New England Contra Dance Music (Kicking Mule 216)
Namour and Smith	Traditional Fiddle Music of Mississippi Vol. 1 (County 528)

Banish Misfortune

How to Change a Flat Tire	A Point of Departure (Front Hall 09)
Trapezoid	Three Forks of Cheat (Rounder 0113)

Barlow Knife

Ebenezer	Tell It to Me (Biograph 6007)
Fuzzy Mountain String Band	Summer Oaks and Porch (Rounder 0035)

Bastringue, La

Beaudoin Family	Same (Philo 2002)
*Jean Carignan	French Canadian Fiddle Songs (Legacy 120)
Frank Ferrel	Fiddle Tunes (Voyager 320-S)

Appears as **La Bastraine.**

Wilfred Guillette	Old Time Fiddlin' (Green Mountain 1061)

Battering Ram, The

How to Change a Flat Tire	A Point of Departure (Front Hall 09)

Battle of Aughrim, The

Chieftains	Chieftains 4 (Claddagh CC14)

Beaumont Rag

Michael Aumen	Kicking Mule's Flat Picking Guitar Festival (Kicking Mule 206)
Berline, Bush, and O'Connor	In Concert (Omac-2)
*Bill Boyd's Cowboy Ramblers	Same (RCA AXM2 5503 – Bluebird reissue)
East Texas Serenaders	1927-1936 (County 410)
Dave Ferguson and Friends	Somewhere over the Rainbow (Ridge Runner 0003)
Bill Long	Mountain Fiddlin' Music from Montana (American Heritage 14)
Tim O'Brien	Guess Who's in Town (Biscuit City 1317)
Mark O'Connor	A Texas Jam Session (Omac-1)
Plank Road String Band	Vocal and Instrumental Blend (June Appal 015)
Buck Ryan	Instrumentals Country Style (Mercury SRW 16261)
Smith's Garage Fiddle Band	Texas Farewell (County 517)
Vernon Solomon	Texas Hoedown (County 703)
*Blaine Sprouse	Same (Rounder 0117)
Marion Sumner	Road to Home (June Appal 030)
Doc Watson	The Essential Doc Watson (Vanguard VSD 45/46)

Bob Wills	30 Fiddler's Greatest Hits (Gusto 104)

Big Mon

*Bobby Hicks	Texas Crapshooter (County 772)
Bill Monroe	Bluegrass Instrumentals (Decca DL 74601)
Tony Rice	Same (Rounder 0085)

Big Sandy River

*Kenny Baker	Kenny Baker Plays Bill Monroe (County 761)
Fiddlin' Van Kidwell	Midnight Ride (Vetco 506)
Bill Monroe	Bluegrass Special (MCA-97—formerly Decca DL7-4382)
Vivian Williams and Barbara Lamb	Twin Sisters (Voyager 316-S)

Bill Cheatham

Kenny Baker	Portrain of a Bluegrass Fiddler (County 719)
John Burke	Fancy Pickin and Plain Singing (Kicking Mule 202)
Vassar Clements	Crossing the Catskills (Rounder 0016)
Kyle Creed	Blue Ridge Style Square Dance (Mountain 301)
Jerry Douglas	Fluxology (Rounder 0093)
Fennig's All-Star String Band	The Hammered Dulcimer Strikes Again (Front Hall 010)
Dave Ferguson and Friends	Somewhere over the Rainbow (Ridge Runner 0003)
Dave Frisbee and Byron Berline	Fiddle Jam Session (Voyager 301)
Carl Jackson	Bluegrass Festival (Prize 498-02)
New Lost City Ramblers	String Band Instrumentals (Folkways 2492)
Marie Rhines	The Reconciliation (Fretless 118)
Arthur Smith	Old-Time Fiddle Classics (County 506)
Roger Sprung	Grassy Licks (Folkways FTS 31036)
Marion Sumner	Road to Home (June Appal 030)

Graham Townsend	Le Violon/The Fiddle (Rounder 7002)
Doc Watson	On Stage (Vanguard VSD 9/10)

Billy in the Lowground

Jana Greif	I Love Fiddlin' (American Heritage 516)
Clark Kessinger	Fiddler (Folkways 2336)
Clark Kessinger	Live at Union Grove (Folkways 2337)
Clark Kessinger	The Legend of Clark Kessinger (County 733)
Mark O'Connor	National Junior Fiddle Champion (Rounder 0046)
Plank Road String Band	Vocal and Instrumental Blend (June Appal 015)
Hubert and Ted Powers	Two Generations of Old Time Fiddle (Mag)
Ola Belle Reed	Same (Rounder 0021)
Doc Roberts	Classic Fiddle Tunes (Davis Unlimited 33015)
Eck Robertson	Master Fiddler (Sonyatone 201)
Lowe Stokes	Old-Time Fiddle Classics (County 507)
Benny Thomasson	You Be the Judge (American Heritage 515)
Benny Thomasson	Texas Hoedown (County 703)
Benny and Jerry Thomasson	A Jam Session (Voyager 309)
Thomasson, Shorty, Morris, and O'Connor	A Texas Jam Session (Omac-1)
Doc Watson	On Stage (Vanguard VSD 9/10)

Black and White Rag

Milton Brown and His Brownies	Beer Parlour Jive (String 801)
Ernie Hunter	All about Fiddling (Stoneway 143)
*Terry Morris	A Texas Jam Session (Omac-1)
Benny Thomasson	Country Fiddling (County 724)

Blackberry Blossom I

Jay Belt	Fiddlin Jay Belt (American Heritage 510)
Curly Ray Cline	Clinch Mountain Boy Jailed (Rebel 1566)

Sonny Miller	Virginia Breakdown (County 705)
Mark O'Connor	A Texas Jam Session (Omac-1)
Mark O'Connor	Markology (Rounder 0090)
Tony Rice	Manzanita (Rounder 0092)
Arthur Smith	Volume 2 (County 547)
Roger Sprung	Progressive Bluegrass Vol. 3 (Folkways FA 2472)
Doc Watson	The Essential Doc Watson (Vanguard VSD 45/46)
The White Brothers	In Sweden (Rounder 0073)

(Blackberry Blossom II)

Mary Bergin	Traditional Irish Music (Shanachie 79006)
James Morrison	The Pure Genius of James Morrison (Shanachie 33004)

(Blackberry Blossom III)

Kevin Burke	An Fhidil Straith II (Gael-Linn 069)

Black Nag, The

*Fennig's All Star String Band	The Hammered Dulcimer (Front Hall 01)
Phil Merrill and Marshall Barron	By Popular Demand (Country Dance Society 6)
Michael and McCreesh	Dance, Like a Wave of the Sea (Front Hall 017)
Jack Walton and Roger Nicholson	Bygone Days (Front Hall 015)

Boatin' Up Sandy

Hollow Rock String Band	Same (Rounder 0024)

Bonaparte Crossing the Rhine

Fuzzy Mountain String Band	Summer Oaks and Porch (Rounder 0035)

Bonaparte Crossing the Rocky Mountains

Bob Carlin	Melodic Clawhammer Banjo (Kicking Mule 209)

Bonaparte's Retreat

Fuzzy Mountain String Band	Same (Rounder 0010)
Tommy Jarrell	Sail Away Ladies (County 756)
Pete Parish	Clawhammer Banjo (Tennvale 003)

Mike Seeger	Old Time Country Music (Folkways FA 2325)	
Arthur Smith	Vol. 1 (County 546)	
Fred Sokolow	Bluegrass Banjo Inventions (Kicking Mule 212)	
Dave Swarbrick	Swarbrick 2 (Transatlantic 341)	
Benny Thomasson	Texas Hoedown (County 703)	
Jay Ungar and Lyn Hardy	Songs, Ballads, and Fiddle Tunes (Philo 1023)	
The Watson Family	The Watson Family Album (Folkways FA 2366)	

Bonnie Isle o' Whalsay

Anderson, Bain, Hunter, and Tulloch	The Silver Bow (Philo 2019)	

Bonnie Kate

*Kevin Burke	Sweeney's Dream (Folkways FW 8876)	
Jean Carignan	Old Time Fiddle Tunes (Folkways FG 3531)	
Jean Carignan	French Canadian Fiddle Songs (Legacy 120)	
James Morrison	The Pure Genius of James Morrison (Shanachie 33004)	

Boys of Bluehill, The

Barry, Gorman, Ennis, and Heaney	Irish Music in London Pubs (Folkways FG 3575)	
Jack Wade	Ceili Music of Ireland (Copley DWL-9-617)	

Briarpicker Brown

*Norman Blake	The Rising Fawn String Ensemble (Rounder 0122)	
Buddy Thomas	Kitty Puss (Rounder 0032)	

Bride's a Bonnie Thing, The

Boys of the Lough	First Album (Trailer LER 2086)	
*Anderson, Bain Hunter, and Tulloch	The Silver Bow (Philo 2019)	

Bull at the Wagon

Earl Collins	That's Earl (Briar 0798)	
*Dempson and Denmon Lewis	Texas Farewell (County 517)	

Bunch of Keys, The I

Barry, Gorman, Ennis, and Heaney	Irish Music in London Pubs (Folkways FG 3575)	
*Kevin Burke	Sweeney's Dream (Folkways FW 8876)	
Jack Wade	Ceili Music from Ireland (Copley DWL-9-617)	

Bunch of Keys II

Appears as **Old Bunch of Keys.**

Cockerham, Jarrell, and Jenkins	Down to the Cider Mill (County 713)	
*Pickin' around the Cookstove	Same (Rounder 0040)	

Campbell's Farewell to Red Gap

Appears as **Steph's Reel**

*Kenny Hall	Same (Philo 1008)	
John McCutcheon	The Wind That Shakes the Barley (June Appal 014)	

Carolan's Concerto

Derek Bell	Carolan's Receipt (Claddagh CC18)	
Chieftains	Chieftains 3 (Island ILPS 9379)	
*Delaware Water Gap	String Band Music (Adelphi 2004)	
Sean McGuire	Ireland's Champion Traditional Fiddler (Outlet 1031)	

Cattle in the Cane

Berline, Bush, and O'Connor	In Concert (Omac-2)	
Norman Blake	Directions (Takoma D-1064)	
Lonnie Peerce	Golden Fiddle Tones (American Heritage 24)	

Appears as **Cattle in the Corn.**

*Joe Greene	Joe Greene's Fiddle Album (County 722)	

Cherokee Shuffle

Norman Blake	Rising Fawn String Ensemble (Rounder 0122)	
Delaware Water Gap	String Band Music (Adelphi AD 2004)	
Fennig's All-Star String Band	Saturday Night in the Provinces (Front Hall 05)	

*Old Reliable String Band	Same (Folkways FA 2475)	Coleraine	
Hubert and Ted Powers	Two Generations of Old Time Fiddle (Mag)	Andy Cahan	Melodic Clawhammer Banjo (Kicking Mule 209)

Chicken Reel

Curly Ray Cline	Chicken Reel (Rebel 1498)	*Fennig's All-Star String Band	The Hammered Dulcimer (Front Hall 01)

Colored Aristocracy

Richard Lieberson and the Central Park Sheiks	Kicking Mule's Flat Picking Guitar Festival (Kicking Mule 206)	Richard Greene	Duets (Rounder 0075)
Charlie Monroe	On the Noonday Jamboree (County 538)	New Lost City Ramblers	Vol. 1 (Folkways FA 2396)
Loyd Wanzer	Plain and Fancy Fiddlin' (American Heritage 19A)	Spark Gap Wonder Boys	Cluck Old Hen (Rounder 0002)
*The Tune Wranglers	Beer Parlour Jive (String 801)	*Fennig's All-Star String Band.	The Hammered Dulcimer (Front Hall 01)
		Yankee Ingenuity	Kitchen Junket (Fretless 200A)

Chief O'Neill's Favorite

Come Dance and Sing

Andy Cahan	Melodic Clawhammer Banjo (Kicking Mule 209)	Delaware Water Gap	String Band Music (Adelphi 2004)
Garrai Eoin II Ceili Band	Irish Music: The Living Tradition, Vol. 2 (Green Linnet 1022)	*Fennig's All-Star String Band	The Hammered Dulcimer (Front Hall 01)

Congress Reel, The

Seán Keane	An Fhidil Sraith II (Gael-Linn CEF 069)	Seamus Creagh	An Fhidil Straith II (Gael-Linn CEF 069)
Sean McGuire	Ireland's Champion Traditional Fiddler (Outlet 1031)	Frankie Gavin	Traditional Music of Ireland (Shenachie 29008)
Dave Swarbrick	Swarbrick 2 (Transatlantic 341)	*The Irish Tradition	The Corner House (Green Linnet 1016)

Chorus Jig

Cooley's Reel

Dave Swarbrick	Swarbrick (Transatlantic 337)	Russ Barenberg	Cowboy Calypso (Rounder 0111)

Cluck Old Hen

Appears as **Joe Cooley's Reel.**

John Ashby	Down on Ashby's Farm (County 745)	Patricia Conway, and Mick Moloney	Irish Music: The Living Tradition (Green Linnet 1009)
The Hill-Billies	Same (County 405)	Frank Ferrel	Fiddle Tunes (Voyager 320-S)
Tommy Jarrell	Sail Away Ladies (County 756)	Marie Rhines	The Reconciliation (Fretless 118)
Bill Long	More Fiddle Jam Sessions (Voyager 304)	Appears as the third tune of the medley **Four Reels.**	
Pete Parish	Clawhammer Banjo (Tennvale 003)	*Jay Ungar and Lyn Hardy	Catskill Mountain Goose Chase (Philo 1040)
Pickin' around the Cookstove	Same (Rounder 0040)		

Cotton Patch Rag

Spark Gap Wonder Boys	Cluck Old Hen (Rounder 0002)	The Dillards with Byron Berline	Pickin' and Fiddlin' (Elektra EKS 7285)
Ora Spiva	More Fiddle Jam Sessions (Voyager 304)	*Lewis Franklin	Texas Fiddle Favorites (County 707)
Roger Sprung	Grassy Licks (Folkways FTS 31036)	Earl Garner	Fiddle Hoedown (Stoneway 148)

Herman Johnson	More Fiddle Jam Sessions (Voyager 304)	
Mark O'Connor	Pickin' in the Wind (Rounder 0068)	
Mark O'Connor	A Texas Jam Session (Omac-1)	
Benny Thomasson	You Be the Judge (American Heritage 515)	
Benny and Jerry Thomasson	A Jam Session (Voyager 309)	

Crazy Creek

Bottle Hill	A Rumor in Their Own Time (Biograph RC6006)
*Delaware Water Gap	From the Rivers of Babylon to the Land of Jazz (Kicking Mule 205)
The Dillards with Byron Berline	Pickin' and Fiddlin' (Elektra EKS 7285)
Bill Keith	Something Auld, Something Newgrass, Something Borrowed, Something Bluegrass
Jack Tottle	Back Road Mandolin (Rounder 0067)
Graham Townsend	Le Violon/The Fiddle (Rounder 7002)

Cricket on the Hearth

*Kenny Baker	Portrait of a Bluegrass Fiddler (County 719)
Jay Belt	Fiddling Jay Belt (American Heritage 510)
John McCutcheon	The Wind That Shakes the Barley (June Appal 014)

Cripple Creek

Appears as **Going Up Cripple Creek.**

*Flatt and Scruggs	Live at Vanderbilt University (Columbia CL 2134)
Albert Nash, Paul Spencer, and Jones Baldwin	Old Originals Vol. II (Rounder 0058)
Mark O'Connor	You Be the Judge (American Heritage 515)
Doc Roberts	Classic Fiddle Tunes (Davis Unlimited 33015)
Vernon Solomon	Texas Hoedown (County 703)
Benny and Jerry Thomasson	A Jam Session (Voyager 309)
Doc Watson	At Folk City (Folkways FA 2426)

Cross Reel

Anderson, Bain, Hunter, and Tulloch	The Silver Bow (Philo 2019)

Cuckoo's Nest

Pat Dunford	The Old-Time Banjo in America (Kicking Mule 204)

Appears as the first tune of **Instrumental Medley.**

Fairport Convention	Angel Delight (A&M SP 4319)
Dan White and John Summers	Fine Times at Our House (Folkways FS 3809)
Ed Haley	Parkersburg Landing (Rounder 1010)
Michael and McCreesh	Dance, Like a Wave of the Sea (Front Hall 017)
Mark O'Connor	National Junior Fiddle Champion (Rounder 0046)
Brother Oswald and Charlie Collins	Oz and Charlie (Rounder 0060)
Jerry Robichaud	Maritime Dance Party (Fretless 201)
Dave Swarbrick and Friends	The Ceilidh Album (Sonet SNTF 764)
Vivian Williams and Barbara Lamb	Twin Sisters (Voyager 316-S)

Cuffey

Highwoods String Band	No. 3 Special (Rounder 0074)

Dailey's Reel

*Kenny Baker	Farmyard Swing County 775)
Joe Greene	Joe Greene's Fiddle Album (County 722)

Dallas Rag

*Dallas String Band	String Ragtime (Yazoo L 1045)
*Dallas String Band	Ragtime 2 (RBF 18)
John McCutcheon	The Wind That Shakes the Barley (June Appal 014)
New Lost City Ramblers	Vol. 1 (Folkways FA 2396)

Dance All Night

John Ashby	Old Virginia Fiddling (County 727)

Curly Ray Cline	Fishin' for Another Hit (Rebel 1531)	
*Highwoods String Band	Dance All Night (Rounder 0045)	
Clark Kessinger	Fiddler (Folkways FA 2336)	
Clark Kessinger	The Legend of Clark Kessinger (County 733)	

Appears as **Give the Fiddler a Dram.**

Lonnie Peerce	Golden Fiddle Tones (American Heritage 24)

Dennis Murphy's Polka

Planxty	Cold Blow and the Rainy Night (Shanachie 79011)
Planxty	Planxty Collection (Polydor 2383 397)

Devil's Dream

Bottle Hill	A Rumor in Their Own Time (Biograph RC6006)
Jean Carignan	French Canadian Fiddle Songs (Legacy 120)
Jana Greif	I Love Fiddlin' (American Heritage 516)
Fiddlin' Red Herron	30 Fiddler's Greatest Hits (Gusto 104)
Clark Kessinger	Sweet Bunch of Daisies (County 747)
Bill Mitchell and Vivian Williams	Fiddle Jam Session (Voyager 301)
Roger Sprung	Grassy Licks (Folkways FTS 31036)
Jay Ungar and Lyn Hardy	Catskill Mountain Goose Chase (Philo 1040)
Eric Weisberg and Marshall Brickman	Folk Banjo Styles (Elektra 217)

Dill Pickle Rag

Dan Crary	Lady's Fancy (Rounder 0099)
Lewis Franklin	Texas Fiddle Favorites (County 707)
Kessinger Brothers	Ragtime 2 (RBF 18)
Clark Kessinger	Live at Union Grove (Folkways FA 2337)
Spark Gap Wonder Boys	Cluck Old Hen (Rounder 0002)
Roger Sprung	Ragtime Bluegrass 2 (Folkways FA 2371)

Done Gone

*Kenny Baker	High Country (County 714)
Ed Haley	Parkersburg Landing (Rounder 1010)
Carl Jackson	Bluegrass Festival (Prize 498-02)
Tommy Jackson	Square Dances without Calls (MCA-162)
Clark Kessinger	Volume 2 (County 747)
Bill Long	Mountain Fiddlin' Music from Montana (American Heritage 14)
Clayton McMichen	Old-Time Fiddle Classics (County 507)
Eck Robertson	Master Fiddler (Sonyatone 201)

Don Tremaine's Reel

Fennig's All-Star String Band	The Hammered Dulcimer (Front Hall 01)

Double File

Alan Block	New England Contra Dance Music (Kicking Mule 216)
*Fuzzy Mountain String Band	Same (Rounder 0010)

Dowd's Favorite

Appears as the third tune of **Cape Breton Medley.**

Jean Carignan	Same (Philo 2001)
Kathleen Collins	Same (Shanachie 29002)
*Steeleye Span	Ten Map Mop (Pegasus Mooncrest 9)

Draggin' the Bow

*Cliff Bruner's Texas Wanderers	Beer Parlour Jive (String 801)

Appears as **Drag That Fiddle.**

Harry Choates	30 Fiddler's Greatest Hits (Gusto 104)
Hickory Wind	At the Wednesday Night Waltz (Adelphi 2002)
Buck Ryan	Draggin' the Bow (Rebel 1552)
Marion Sumner	Road to Home (June Appal 030)

Benny and Jerry Thomasson	A Jam Session (Voyager 309)		Clark Kessinger	Volume 2 (County 747)
?	25 Old Tyme Fiddle Hits (K-Tel FH1)		Grant Lamb	Tunes from Home (Voyager 312-S)

Drowsy Maggie

Chieftains	Chieftains 4 (Claddagh CC14)		Lonnie Peerce	Golden Fiddle Tones (American Heritage 24)
Frankie Gavin	Traditional Music of Ireland (Shanachie 29008)		*Red Clay Ramblers	Same (Folkways FTS 31039)
Hickory Wind	At the Wednesday Night Waltz (Adelphi 2002)		Benny and Jerry Thomasson	A Jam Session (Voyager 309)
Marie Rhines	The Reconciliation (Fretless 118)		David Winston	Southern Clawhammer Banjo (Kicking Mule 213)
Dave Swarbrick	Swarbrick (Transatlantic 337)			

Drunken Billy Goat

Durham's Bull

The Dillards with Byron Berline	Pickin' and Fiddlin' (Elektra EKS 7285)		*Lyman Enloe	Fiddle Tunes I Recall (County 762)
Poor Richard's Almanac	Same (American Heritage 25)		Fiddlin' Van Kidwell	Midnight Ride (Vetco 506)

Dubuque

Bob Carlin	Melodic Clawhammer Banjo (Kicking Mule 209)		Hubert and Ted Powers	Two Generations of Old Time Fiddle (Mag)
*Fennig's All-Star String Band	The Hammered Dulcimer (Front Hall 01)		Joe Robichaud	Old Time Fiddler's Contest 7/26/75 (Green Mountain 1050)

Ducks on the Millpond I

Tommy Jarrell	Come and Go with Me (County 748)		Spark Gap Wonder Boys	Cluck Old Hen (Rounder 0002)
*Fuzzy Mountain String Band	Summer Oaks and Porch (Rounder 0035)		Paul Warren	America's Greatest Breakdown Fiddle Player (CMH 6237)

(Ducks on the Millpond II)

Dusty Miller I

Kenny Baker	Grassy Fiddle Blues (County 750)		*Fuzzy Mountain String Band	Summer Oaks and Porch (Rounder 0035)

Ducks on the Pond

*Red Clay Ramblers	Same (Folkways FTS 31039)		Eric Thompson	Kicking Mule's Flat Picking Guitar Festival (Kicking Mule 206)

(Dusty Miller IIA)

Oscar and Eugene Wright	Old-Time Fiddle (Rounder 0089)		J.P. and Annadeene Fraley	Wild Rose of the Mountain (Rounder 0037)

Durang's Hornpipe

Dusty Miller IIB

Earl Collins	That's Earl (Briar 0798)		Joe Greene	Joe Greene's Fiddle Album (County 722)
Junior Daugherty	You Be the Judge (American Heritage 515)		Herman Johnson	Champion Fiddlin' (American Heritage 1)
The Dillards with Byron Berline	Pickin' and Fiddlin' (Elektra EKS 7285)		Terry Morris	A Texas Jam Session (Omac-1)
Major Franklin	Texas Fiddle Favorites (County 707)		Mark O'Connor	National Junior Fiddle Champion (Rounder 0046)
			Poor Richard's Almanac	Same (American Heritage 25)
Clark Kessinger	Live at Union Grove (Folkways FA 2337)		*Butch Robbins	Forty Years Late (Rounder 0086)
			Ace Sewell	Southwest Fiddlin' (Voyager 319-S)

Benny Thomasson	Country Fiddling (County 724)
Benny Thomasson	You Be the Judge (American Heritage 515)
Paul Warren	American's Greatest Breakdown Fiddle Player (CMH 6237)

(Dusty Miller IIC)

Bill Monroe	Blue Grass Time (MCA 116 – formerly Decca DL7-4896)

East Tennessee Blues

*Bobby Hicks	Texas Crapshooter (County 772)
Old Reliable String Band	Same (Folkways FA 2475)
Ted Powers	Old Time Fiddler (Mag 1018)
Jim Widner	Fiddle Jam Session (Voyager 301)

Ebenezer

Fuzzy Mountain String Band	Same (Rounder 0010)

Eighth of January

Arkansas Barefoot Boys	Echoes of the Ozarks, Vol. 1 (County 518)
John Ashby	Old Virginia Fiddling (County 727)
Jay Belt	Fiddlin' Jay Belt (American Heritage 510)
Ted Gossett's Band	Old-Time Fiddle Classics, Vol. 2 (County 527)
Bill Long and Ora Spiva	More Fiddle Jam Sessions (Voyager 304)
Tom Paley	Folk Banjo Styles (Elektra 217)
Tony Rice	Same (Rounder 0085)
Buck Ryan	Fiddler on the Rocks (Rebel 1528)

Appears as the first tune of **Fiddle Tune Medley.**

Buddy Spicher	Me and My Heroes (Flying Fish 065)
Scotty Stoneman	Live in L.A. (Brian 4206)
Pete Sutherland	An Anthology (Tennvale 004)
Graham Townsend	Le Violon/The Fiddle (Rounder 7002)

Paul Warren	America's Greatest Breakdown Fiddle Player (CMH 6237)

Elzic's Farewell

Wilson Douglas	The Right Hand Fork of Rush's Creek (Rounder 0047)
Pickin' around the Cookstove	Same (Rounder 0040)
Tommy Thompson	The Old-Time Banjo in America (Kicking Mule 204)
Wretched Refuse	Same (Beet 7003)

Fairy Dance

Cape Breton Symphony	Fiddle (Glencoe 001)
Winnie Chafe	Highland Melodies (Rounder 7012)
*Dave Swarbrick	Swarbrick 2 (Transatlantic 341)

Fire on the Mountain

Fuzzy Mountain String Band	Summer Oaks and Porch (Rounder 0035)
*Highwoods String Band	Fire on the Mountain (Rounder 0023)
E.J. Hopkins	Fiddle Hoedown (Stoneway 148 148)
The Kentucky Colonels	Living in the Past (Briar 4202)
Benny Martin	The Fiddle Collection (CMH 9006)

Appears as the third tune of **Fiddle Tune Medley.**

Buddy Spicher	Me and My Heroes (Flying Fish 065)

Fisher's Hornpipe

Jean Carignan	Old Time Fiddle Tunes (Folkways FG 3531)
Joseph Cormier	The Dances Down Home (Rounder 7004)
The Dillards with Byron Berline	Pickin' and Fiddlin' (Elektra EKS 7285)
John Francis	You Be the Judge (American Heritage 515)
Major Franklin	Texas Fiddle Favorites (County 707)
Fuzzy Mountain String Band	Summer Oaks and Porch (Rounder 0035)
The Hill-Billies	Same (County 405)
Tommy Jarrell	Sail Away Ladies (County 756)

Bill Mitchell and Vivian Williams	More Fiddle Jam Sessions (Voyager 304)
Marie Rhines	The Reconciliation (Fretless 118)
Buddy Spicher	American Sampler (Flying Fish 021)
Roger Sprung	Progressive Bluegrass, Vol. 3 (Folkways FA 2472)
Sumner and McReynolds	Old Friends (Mag 3901)
Jack Tottle	Back Road Mandolin (Rounder 0067)

Flop-Eared Mule

Glenn Feener	Old Time Fiddler's Contest 7/30/77 (Green Mountain 1062)
Carl Jackson	Bluegrass Festival (Prize 498-02)
Clark Kessinger	Fiddler (Folkways FA 2336)
Clark Kessinger	The Legend of Clark Kessinger (County 733)
Sonja Nordstrom	Old Time Fiddling 1976 (Fretless 122)
Ted Powers	Old Time Fiddler (Mag 1018)
Ola Belle Reed	Same (Rounder 0021)
Reno and Smiley	Banjo Special (King 787)
Eric Weisberg and Marshall Brickman	Folk Banjo Styles (Elektra 217)
Don Wiles, Jim Widner, and Vivian Williams	Fiddle Jam Session (Voyager 301)

Flowers of Edinburgh A

Cape Breton Symphony	Fiddle (Glencoe 001)
Paul Chrisman	Old Time Fiddler's Contest 7/26/75 (Green Mountain 1050)
*Fennig's All-Star String Band	The Hammered Dulcimer (Front Hall 01)
Rufus Guinchard	Newfoundland Fiddler (Breakwater 1002)
Kenny Hall	Same (Philo 1008)
Hickory Wind	At the Wednesday Night Waltz (Adelphi 2002)
Ken Perlman	Melodic Clawhammer Banjo (Kicking Mule 209)

| The Scottish Fiddle Festival Orchestra | Scottish Traditional Fiddle Music (Olympic 6151) |

(Flowers of Edinburgh B)

| Dave Swarbrick and Friends | The Ceilidh Album (Sonet 764) |

Flying Cloud Cotillon

| Bob Carlin | Melodic Clawhammer Banjo (Kicking Mule 209) |

Folding Down the Sheets

| Bob Carlin | Melodic Clawhammer Banjo (Kicking Mule 209) |

Forked Deer

| Charlie Bowman and His Brothers | Old-Time Fiddle Classics, Vol. 2 (County 527) |

Appears as **Forked Buck.**

Wilson Douglas	The Right Hand Fork of Rush's Creek (Rounder 0047)
*J.P. and Annadeene Fraley	Wild Rose of the Mountain (Rounder 0037)
Major Franklin	Texas Fiddle Favorites (County 707)
Ed Haley	Parkersburg Landing (Rounder 1010)
*Highwoods String Band	Dance All Night (Rounder 0045)
Ernie Hunter	All about Fiddling (Stoneway 143)
Ernie Hunter	Fiddle Hoedown (Stoneway 148)
Thomas Hunter	Deep in Tradition (June Appal 007)
Tommy Jarrell	Sail Away Ladies (County 756)
Fiddlin' Van Kidwell	Midnight Ride (Vetco 506)
New Lost City Ramblers	Vol. 1 (Folkways FA 2396)
John Rector	Old Originals, Vol. II (Rounder 0058)
Roger Sprung	Progressive Bluegrass, Vol. 3 (Folkways FA 2472)
Vivian Williams and Barbara Lamb	Twin Sisters (Voyager 316-S)

Frieze Breeches

| Paddy Cronin | Kerry's Own (Outlet 3002) |

Glinside Ceili Band | Irish Music: The Living Tradition (Green Linnet 1009)

Appears as part of the song **Cunla**.

*Planxty | Planxty Collection (Polydor 2383 397)

Jody Stecher | Snake Baked a Hoecake (Bat 203)

Appears as **Friar's Breeches**.

Dave Swarbrick | Swarbrick 2 (Transatlantic 341)

Jack Wade | Ceili Music from Ireland (Copley DWL-9-617)

Frosty Morning

Fuzzy Mountain String Band | Same (Rounder 0010)

Galley Watch, Da

*Boys of the Lough | Second Album (Rounder 3006)

Hunter and Tulloch | The Silver Bow (Philo 2019)

Gallopede

Fennig's All-Star String Band | Saturday Night in the Provinces (Front Hall 05)

Gaspé Reel

Louis Beaudoin | Same (Philo 2000)

Joe Gagne | Old Time Fiddler's Contest 7/26/75 (Green Mountain 1050)

Henry Sapoznik | Melodic Clawhammer Banjo (Kicking Mule 209)

Matthew Smith | Old Time Fiddling 1976 (Fretless 122)

Fennig's All-Star String Band | The Hammered Dulcimer (Front Hall 01)

Wretched Refuse | Same (Beet 7003)

Girl I Left behind Me, The

Fuzzy Mountain String Band | Same (Rounder 0010)

Dick Gordon | Old Time Fiddler's Contest 7/26/75 (Green Mountain 1050)

Hubert and Ted Powers | Powers Town Music (Mag)

Give the Fiddler a Dram I

The Carter Brothers and Son | Echoes of the Ozarks, Vol. 1 (County 518)

Appears as **Fiddler a Dram**.

Country Cooking | Fourteen Bluegrass Instrumentals (Rounder 0006)

(Give the Fiddler a Dram II)

Pete Sutherland | An Anthology (Tennvale 004)

Golden Slippers

John Burke | The Old-Time Banjo in America (Kicking Mule 204)

Delaware Water Gap | Fox Hollow String Band Festival (Biograph 6008)

Clark Kessinger | Live at Union Grove (Folkways FA 2337)

*Fennig's All-Star String Band | The Hammered Dulcimer (Front Hall 01)

Buddy Pendleton | Virginia Breakdown (County 705)

Ted Powers | Old Time Fiddler (Mag 1018)

Buck Ryan | Draggin' the Bow (Rebel 1552)

Sumner and McReynolds | Old Friends (Mag 3901)

Gold Ring, The

*Boys of the Lough | Second Album (Rounder 3006)

Seán Keane | Gusty's Frolicks (Claddagh CC17)

Matt Molloy | Same (Mulligan 004)

Goldrush

Berline, Bush, and O'Connor | In Concert (Omac-2)

*Bill Monroe | Country Music Hall of Fame (MCA 140 — formerly Decca D17-5281)

Marion Sumner | Road to Home (June Appal 030)

Jay Ungar and Lyn Hardy | Songs, Ballads, and Fiddle Tunes (Philo 1023)

Wretched Refuse | Same (Beet 7003)

Goodbye Liza Jane

    Kyle Creed   Blue Ridge Style Square
Dance Time
(Mountain 301)

    Appears as **Liza Jane.**

    Delaware Water Gap   From the Rivers of Baby
lon to the Land of Jazz
(Kicking Mule 205)

    *Bobby Hicks   Texas Crapshooter
(County 772)

    Reno and Smiley   Banjo Special
(King 787)

    Bob Wills and Mel
Tillis   Mel Tillis and Bob Wills
In Person
(Kapp KS 3639)

Gravel Walk, The

    *Boys of the Lough   Second Album
(Rounder 3006)

    Patricia Conway and
Mick Maloney   Irish Music: The Living
Tradition
(Green Linnet 1009)

Greenfields of America

    *Andy Cahan   Melodic Clawhammer
Banjo
(Kicking Mule 209)

    Michael Coleman   The Legacy of Michael
Coleman
(Shanachie 33002)

    Fennig's All-Star
String Band   Saturday Night in the
Provinces
(Front Hall 010)

    Tom Gilfellon   Kicking Mule's Flat
Picking Guitar Festival
(Kicking Mule 206)

    Appears as **Charming
Molly Brannigan.**

    Art Rosenbaum   Five String Banjo
(Kicking Mule 208)

Green Willis

    Bob Carlin and
Henry Sapoznik   Melodic Clawhammer
Banjo
(Kicking Mule 209)

    *Fuzzy Mountain
String Band   Same
(Rounder 0010)

Grey Eagle

    *Kenny Baker   Dry and Dusty
(County 744)

    Byron Berline   Dad's Favorites
(Rounder 0100)

    Earl Collins   That's Earl
(Briar 0798)

    Dan Crary   Lady's Fancy
(Rounder 0099)

    Dave Ferguson and
Friends   Somewhere over the
Rainbow
(Ridge Runner 0003)

    Joe Greene   Joe Greene's Fiddle
Album
(County 722)

    Jana Greif   I Love Fiddlin'
(American Heritage 516)

    Thomas Hunter   Deep in Tradition
(June Appal 007)

    Herman Johnson   Champion Fiddling
(American Heritage 1)

    Bill Long   Fiddle Jam Session
(Voyager 301)

    Sonny Miller   Virginia Breakdown
(County 705)

    Mark O'Connor   Pickin' in the Wind
(Rounder 0068)

    Lonnie Peerce   Golden Fiddle Tones
(American Heritage 24)

    Bartow Riley   Texas Hoedown
(County 703)

    Butch Robbins   Forty Years Late
(Rounder 0086)

    Art Rosenbaum   Five String Banjo
(Kicking Mule 208)

    Ace Sewell   Southwest Fiddlin'
(Voyager 319-S)

    Benny and Jerry
Thomasson   A Jam Session
(Voyager 309)

    Paul Warren   America's Greatest
Breakdown Fiddle
Player
(CMH 6237)

**Growling Old Man and
Woman, The**

    Kenny Baker   Frost on the Pumpkin
(County 770)

    Louis Beaudoin   Same
(Philo 2000)

    Delaware Water Gap   String Band Music
(Adelphi AD2004)

    Ebenezer   Fox Hollow String Band
Festival
(Biograph 6008)

    Appears as **The Old
Man and the Old
Woman.**

    Jerry Holland   Same
(Rounder 7008)

    The Riendeau Family   Old-Time Fiddling
(County 725)

    Yankee Ingenuity   Kitchen Junket
(Fretless 200A)

Hamilton County

The Dillards with Byron Berline	Pickin' and Fiddlin' (Elektra EKS 7285)

Harvest Home

Fennig's All-Star String Band	The Hammered Dulcimer (Front Hall 01)
Sean McGuire	Ireland's Champion Traditional Fiddler (Sonet 1031)
Dave Swarbrick and Friends	The Ceilidh Album (Sonet 764)
Jack Wade	Ceili Music from Ireland (Copley DWL-9-617)

Haste to the Wedding

Jean Carignan	Old Time Fiddle Tunes (Folkways FG 3531)
*Fennig's All-Star String Band	The Hammered Dulcimer (Front Hall 01)
?	25 Old Tyme Fiddle Hits (K-Tel FH1)

Hawkin's Rag

New Lost City Ramblers	Vol. 2 (Folkways FA 2397)
New Lost City Ramblers	On the Great Divide (Folkways FTS 31041)

Hell among the Yearlings

Curly Ray Cline	Fishin' for Another Hit (Rebel 1531)
*Country Cooking	Fourteen Bluegrass Instrumentals (Rounder 0006)
*Clark Kessinger	Fiddler (Folkways FA 2336)
*Clark Kessinger	The Legend of Clark Kessinger (County 733)
Fiddlin' Van Kidwell	Midnight Ride (Vetco 506)
Bill Mitchell	Fiddle Jam Session (Voyager 301)
Hubert and Ted Powers	Two Generations of Old Time Fiddle (Mag)
Fred Sokolow	Bluegrass Banjo Inventions (Kicking Mule 209)
Vivian Williams and Barbara Lamb	Twin Sisters (Voyager 316-S)
Wretched Refuse	Fox Hollow String Band Festival (Biograph 6008)

Hog Eye

New Lost City Ramblers	Vol. 3 (Folkways FA 2398)
Pope's Arkansas Mountaineers	Echoes of the Ozarks, Vol. 1 (County 518)

Hunter's Purse, The

*Arm and Hammer String Band	New England Contra Dance Music (Kicking Mule 216)
Kevin Burke	If the Cap Fits (Mulligan LUN 021)
Chieftains	Chieftains 3 (Island ILPS 9379)
Jack Wade	Ceili Music from Ireland (Copley DWL-9-617)

Jack Broke da Prison Door

Anderson, Bain, Hunter, and Tulloch	The Silver Bow (Philo 2019)

Jackson Stomp

New Lost City Ramblers	String Band Instrumentals (Folkways FA 2492)

Jaybird

Country Cooking	Fourteen Bluegrass Instrumentals (Rounder 0006)
*Fennig's All-Star String Band	Saturday Night in the Provinces (Front Hall 05)

Jenny Lind Polka

*Hollow Rock String Band	Same (Rounder 0024)

Appears as **Heel and Toe Polka.**

Bill Monroe	Uncle Pen (MCA DL7-5348)
The Old Virginia Fiddlers	Rare Recordings (County 201)

Johnny the Blacksmith I

Kenny Baker	Baker's Dozen (County 730)

(Johnny the Blacksmith II)

Fennig's All-Star String Band	The Hammered Dulcimer Strikes Again (Front Hall 010)

John Ryan's Polka

    Planxty   Cold Blow and the
                            Rainy Night
                            (Shanachie 79011)

    Planxty   Planxty Collection
                            (Polydor 2382 397)

Joys of Quebec

    Jerry Rivers   30 Fiddler's Greatest
                            Hits
                            (Gusto 104)

    *Yankee Ingenuity   Kitchen Junket
                            (Fretless 200A)

June Apple

    Cockerham, Jarrell,   Down to the Cider Mill
    and Jenkins   (County 713)

    *Red Clay Ramblers   Galax 73
                            (Tennvale 002)

    Roger Sprung and   Bluegrass Blast
    Hal Wylie   (Folkways FTS 31038)

Katy Did

    Lowe Stokes   Hell Broke Loose in
                            Georgia
                            (County 514)

Katy Hill

    John Ashby   Down on Ashby's Farm
                            (County 745)

    *Kenny Baker   Grassy Fiddle Blues
                            (County 750)

    The Carroll County   Same
    Ramblers   (Adelphi 2006)

    Curly Ray Cline   Clinch Mountain Boy
                            Jailed
                            (Rebel 1566)

    Joe Greene   Joe Greene's Fiddle
                            Album
                            (County 722)

    David Guskov   Old Time Fiddler's
                            Contest 7/26/75
                            (Green Mountain 1050)

    Bill Long   Fiddle Jam Session
                            (Voyager 301)

    Bill Monroe   The Father of Blue
                            Grass Music
                            (RCA Camden CAL-719)

    Appears as **Going
    around the World.**

    Charlie Monroe   On the Noonday
                            Jamboree—1944
                            (County 538)

    Paul Warren   America's Greatest
                            Breakdown Fiddle
                            Player
                            (CMH 6237)

    Vivian Williams and   Twin Sisters
    Barbara Lamb   (Voyager 316-S)

    Oscar and Eugene   Old-Time Fiddle
    Wright   (Rounder 0089)

Kesh Jig, The

    The Bothy Band   1975
                            (Mulligan 002)

    The Bothy Band   Afterhours
                            (Mulligan 030)

    Appears as **Kincora
    Jig**

    *Boys of the Lough   Live
                            (Philo 1026)

    Frank Ferrel and   Fiddle Tunes
    Graham Townsend   (Voyager 320-S)

    Sean McGuire   Ireland's Champion
                            Traditional Fiddler
                            (Outlet 1031)

King of the Fairies

    Kevin Burke   Sweeney's Dream
                            (Folkways FW 8876)

    David Curry   My Ireland
                            (Capitol T10028)

    *Dave Swarbrick   Swarbrick 2
                            (Transatlantic 341)

Kitchen Girl, The

    David Bromberg   Kicking Mule's Flat
                            Picking Guitar Festival
                            (Kicking Mule 206)

    *Highwoods String   No. 3 Special
    Band   (Rounder 0074)

    John McCutcheon   The Wind That Shakes
                            the Barley
                            (June Appal 014)

    Oscar and Eugene   Old-Time Fiddle
    Wright   (Rounder 0089)

Lark in the Morning

    Jack Wade   Ceili Music from Ireland
                            (Copley DWL-9-617)

Lasses Trust in Providence

    Anderson, Bain,   The Silver Bow
    Hunter, and Tulloch (Philo 2019)

Last of Callahan, The

    Fuzzy Mountain   Same
    String Band   (Rounder 0010)

    *Highwoods String   Fire on the Mountain
    Band   (Rounder 0023)

Leather Britches

Kenny Baker and Joe Greene	High Country (County 714)
Curly Ray Cline	Chicken Reel (Rebel 1498)
Flatt and Scruggs	Live at Vanderbilt University (Columbia CL 2134)
Lewis Franklin	Texas Fiddle Favorites (County 707)
Hollow Rock String Band	Same (Rounder 0024)
Clark Kessinger	Fiddler (Folkways FA 2336)
Clark Kessinger	The Legend of Clark Kessinger (County 733)
Bill Long	Fiddle Jam Session (Voyager 301)
Bill Long, Bill Mitchell, and Vivian Williams	More Fiddle Jam Sessions (Voyager 304)
Tim O'Brien	Guess Who's in Town (Biscuit City 1317)
The Old Virginia Fiddlers	Rare Recordings (County 201)
Mike Seeger	Same (Vanguard VRS 9150)
The Skillet Lickers	Old Time Tunes (County 506)
Luke Smathers String Band	Mountain Swing (June Appal 024)
Benny and Jerry Thomasson	A Jam Session (Voyager 309)
Paul Warren	America's Greatest Breakdown Fiddle Player (CMH 6237)
Vivian Williams and Barbara Lamb	Twin Sisters (Voyager 316-S)
Johnnie Lee Wills	Tulsa Swing (Rounder 1027)

Lee Highway Blues

Appears as **New Lee Highway Blues.**

David Bromberg	Wanted Dead or Alive (Columbia KC 32717)

Appears as **Lee Highway Ramble**

Ken Clark	30 Fiddler's Greatest Hits (Gusto 104)
Curly Ray Cline	Fishin' for Another Hit (Rebel 1531)

*Highwoods String Band	Fire on the Mountain (Rounder 0023)
The Kentucky Colonels	1965-1967 (Rounder 0070)
Spark Gap Wonder Boys	Cluck Old Hen (Rounder 0002)
Jody Stecher	Snake Baked a Hoecake (Bay 203)

Appears as **Talkin' Fiddle Blues.**

Scotty Stoneman	30 Fiddler's Greatest Hits (Gusto 104)

Appears as **Opry Fiddler's Blues.**

Chubby Wise	30 Fiddler's Greatest Hits (Gusto 104)

Appears as **Hitchhiker Blues.**

?	25 Old Tyme Fiddle Hits (K-Tel FH1)

Lerwick Lasses, Da

Boys of the Lough	Second Album (Rounder 3006)

Liberty

Hershal Brown's Washboard Band	Georgia Fiddle Bands, Vol. 2 (County 544)
Vassar Clements	Crossing the Catskills (Rounder 0016)
Ken Danforth	Old Time Fiddlers' Contest 7/26/75 (Green Mountain 1050)
Fennig's All-Star String Band	The Hammered Dulcimer Strikes Again (Front Hall 010)
Mike Gareau	Old Time Fiddlers' Contest 7/30/77 (Green Mountain 1062)
Art Rosenbaum	Five String Banjo (Kicking Mule 208)
Loyd Wanzer	Plain and Fancy Fiddlin' (American Heritage 19A)
Paul Warren	America's Greatest Breakdown Fiddle Player (CMH 6237)

Little Liza Jane

Ebenezer	Tell It to Me (Biograph 6007)
*J.P. and Annadeene Fraley	Wild Rose of the Mountain (Rounder 0037)

Little Rabbit

Richard Greene — Duets (Rounder 0075)

Michael and McCreesh — Dance, Like a Wave of the Sea (Front Hall 017)

Appears as **Rabbit Where's Your Mammy.**

Tom Paley — Folk Banjo Styles (Elektra 217)

Appears as **Rabbit Where's Your Mammy.**

Pickin' around the Cookstove — Same (Rounder 0040)

Roger Sprung and Hal Wylie — Bluegrass Blast (Folkways FTS 31038)

Loch Lavan Castle

Norman Blake — Directions (Takoma D-1064)

*Fuzzy Mountain String Band — Summer Oaks and Porch (Rounder 0035)

Jerry Holland — Same (Rounder 7008)

Lord Inchiquin

Chieftains — Chieftains 3 (Island ILPS 9379)

Dave Swarbrick — Swarbrick 2 (Transatlantic 341)

Lost Indian I

*Kenny Baker — Farmyard Swing (County 775)

Curly Ray Cline — My Little Home in West Virginia (Rebel 1515)

Clark Kessinger — Old-Time Music (Rounder 0004)

Appears as the second tune of **Fiddle Tune Medley.**

Buddy Spicher — Me and My Heroes (Flying Fish 065)

Sumner and McReynolds — Old Friends (Mag 3901)

Chubby Wise — Fiddle Hoedown (Stoneway 148)

(Lost Indian II)

Byron Berline — Fiddle Jam Session (Voyager 301)

Mose Coffman — Shaking down the Acorns (Rounder 0018)

*Ed Haley — Parkersburg Landing (Rounder 1010)

*Ship in the Clouds — Old Time Instrumental Music (Folkways 31062)

Ora Spiva — More Fiddle Jam Sessions (Voyager 304)

Benny Thomasson — Country Fiddling (County 724)

Louie's First Tune

Ebenezer — Tell It to Me (Biograph 6007)

*The Riendeau Family — Old Time Fiddling (County 725)

Maggie Brown's Favorite

Jerry Holland — Same (Rounder 7008)

Eugene O'Donnell — Slow Airs and Set Dances (Green Linnet 1015)

Magpie

Fuzzy Mountain String Band — Same (Rounder 0010)

Maid behind the Bar, The

*Frank Ferrel — Fiddle Tunes (Voyager 320-S)

Michael and Andrew Carnase — Irish Music: The Living Tradition, Vol. 2 (Green Linnet 1022)

Matt Molloy — Same (Mulligan 004)

Mason's Apron

*Boys of the Lough — Second Album (Rounder 3006)

Kevin Burke — If the Cap Fits (Mulligan LUN 021)

Kevin Burke — Sweeney's Dream (Folkways FW 8876)

Cape Breton Symphony — Fiddle (Glencoe 001)

Jean Carignan — French Canadian Fiddle Songs (Legacy 120)

Reed Kaynor — Old Time Fiddlers' Contest 7/30/77 (Green Mountain 1062)

Sean McGuire — Ireland's Champion Traditional Fiddler (Outlet 1031)

Graham Townsend — Le Violon/The Fiddle (Rounder 7002)

Vivian Williams and Barbara Lamb	Twin Sisters (Voyager 316-S)	

Merrily Kiss the Quaker

*Boys of the Lough	Second Album (Rounder 3006)
Chieftains	Chieftains 3 (Island ILPS 9379)
Tom Gilfellon	Kicking Mule's Flat Picking Guitar Festival (Kicking Mule 206)
Planxty	Same (Shanachie 79009)
Planxty	Planxty Collection (Polydor 2383 397)

Midnight on the Water

Mark O'Connor	Pickin' in the Wind (Rounder 0068)
Fennig's All-Star String Band	The Hammered Dulcimer (Front Hall 01)
*Jay Ungar and Lyn Hardy	Songs, Ballads, and Fiddle Tunes (Philo 1023)
Benny Thomasson	Country Fiddling (County 724)

Miller's Reel A

Alistair Anderson	Traditional Tunes (Front Hall 08)
Byron Berline	Dad's Favorites (Rounder 0100)
Norman Solomon	Texas Fiddle Favorites (County 707)
Red Clay Ramblers	Same (Folkways FTS 31039)

(Miller's Reel B)

J.P. and Annadeene Fraley	Wild Rose of the Mountain (Rounder 0037)

Appears as the first tune of **Four Reels**.

Jay Ungar and Lyn Hardy	Catskill Mountain Goose Chase (Philo 1040)

Mineola Rag

Delaware Water Gap	String Band Music (Adelphi 2004)
*East Texas Serenaders	1927-1936 (County 410)
*East Texas Serenaders	Old-Time Fiddle Classics, Vol. 2 (County 527)

Mississippi Sawyer

Fennig's All-Star String Band	The Hammered Dulcimer (Front Hall 01)

Fiddlin' Van Kidwell	Same (Vetco 502)
John McCutcheon	The Wind That Shakes the Barley (June Appal 014)
New River Ramblers	Galax 73 (Tennvale 002)
The Old Virginia Fiddlers	Rare Recordings (County 201)
Art Rosenbaum	The Art of the Mountain Banjo (Kicking Mule 203)
Gid Tanner and the Skillet Lickers	The Kickapoo Medicine Show (Rounder 1023)

Miss McLeod's Reel

Appears as **Hop Up Ladies**.

The Bogtrotters	The Original Bogtrotters (Biograph 6003)
Cape Breton Symphony	Fiddle (Glencoe 001)
The Carroll County Ramblers	Same (Adelphi 2006)

Appears as **Hop Light Ladies**.

Frank Dalton and George Wood	Old Originals Vol. I (Rounder 0057)

Appears as **Hop Light Ladies**.

Bob Douglas	Old Time Dance Tunes from Sequatchie Valley (Tennvale 001S)
Thomas Hunter	Deep in Tradition (June Appal 007)

Appears as **Hop Light Ladies**.

The Old Virginia Fiddlers	Rare Recordings (County 201)
Pete Parish	Clawhammer Banjo (Tennvale 003)

Appears as **Did You Ever See the Devil, Uncle Joe?**

John Patterson	Old Originals, Vol. II (Rounder 0058)

Appears as **Did You Ever See the Devil, Uncle Joe?**

Doc Roberts	Classic Fiddle Tunes (Davis Unlimited 33015)
Joe Shannon and Johnny McGreevy	The Noonday Feast (Green Linnet 1023)
*Dave Swarbrick	Swarbrick 2 (Transatlantic 341)

Patrick J. Touhey	The Wheels of the World (Shanachie 33001)		

Appears as **Hop Light Ladies**.

Paul Warren	America's Greatest Breakdown Fiddle Player (CMH 6237)

Molly Put the Kettle On I

Haywood Blevins	Old Originals, Vol. II (Rounder 0058)
Ebenezer	Fox Hollow String Band Festival (Biograph 6008)
Leake County Revelers	Traditional Fiddle Music of Mississippi, Vol. 2 (County 529)
New Lost City Ramblers	Vol. 4 (Folkways FA 2399)

Appears as **Polly Put the Kettle On**.

Pickin' around the Cookstove	Same (Rounder 0040)

Appears as **Polly Put the Kettle On**.

Ship in the Clouds	Old Time Instrumental Music (Folkways 31062)
*The Skillet Lickers	Old Time Tunes (County 506)

(Molly Put the Kettle On II)

Ship in the Clouds	Old Time Instrumental Music (Folkways 31062)

Money Musk A

Jean Carignan	Hommage à Joseph Allard (Philo 2012)
*Delaware Water Gap	String Band Music (Adelphi 2004)
Thomas Hunter	Deep in Tradition (June Appal 007)

Money Musk B

*Highwoods String Band	Dance All Night (Rounder 0045)
Marie Rhines	The Reconciliation (Fretless 118)

(Money Musk C)

Joe Greene	Joe Greene's Fiddle Album (County 722)

Monroe's Hornpipe

Kenny Baker	Kenny Baker Plays Bill Monroe (County 761)
Byron Berline	Fiddle Jam Session (Voyager 301)
*Bill Monroe	Bluegrass Instrumentals (Decca 74601)

Morgan Magan

*Chieftains	Chieftains 4 (Claddagh CC14)
Fennig's All-Star String Band	Saturday Night in the Provinces (Front Hall) 05
Dave Swarbrick	Swarbrick 2 (Transatlantic 341)
Trapezoid	Three Forks of Cheat (Rounder 0113)

Morning Dew, The

*Chieftains	Chieftains 4 (Claddagh CC14)
Michael Coleman	The Classic Recordings of Michael Coleman (Shanachie 33006)
Kathleen Collins	Same (Shanachie 29002)
Steeleye Span	Ten Man Mop (Mooncrest Pegasus 9)

Morpeth Rant

*Alistair Anderson	Traditional Tunes (Front Hall 08)
John McCutcheon	The Wind That Shakes the Barley (June Appal 014)

Muddy Roads

Roger Sprung	Grassy Licks (Folkways FTS 31036)
The Watson Family	Same (Folkways FA 2366)

Munster Buttermilk

Appears as **Behind the Haystack**.

*Boys of the Lough	Live (Philo 1026)
Matt Molly, Paul Brady, and Tommy Peoples	Same (Mulligan LUN 017)

Musical Priest, The

Alistair Anderson	Traditional Tunes (Front Hall 08)

James Morrison	The Pure Genius of James Morrison (Shanachie 33004)	
Trapezoid	Three Forks of Cheat (Rounder 0113)	

Nine Points of Roguery, The

Boys of the Lough	Live (Philo 1026)	
*Boys of the Lough	Same (Trailer 2086)	
Tommy Peoples and Paul Brady	The High Part of the Road (Shanachie 29003)	

Nonesuch

Dave Swarbrick	Lift the Lid and Listen (Sonet 763)	
Trapezoid	Three Forks of Cheat (Rounder 0113)	

Off She Goes

Barry, Gorman, Ennis, and Heaney	Irish Music in London Pubs (Folkways FG 3575)	
Fennig's All-Star String Band	Saturday Night in the Provinces (Front Hall 05)	

Appears as **Lancer's Quadrille.**

Donald Perkins	Old Time Fiddling 1976 (Fretless 122)	

Old French

Kenny Hall	Same (Philo 1008)	

Old Joe Clark

Cockerham, Jarrell, and Jenkins	Back Home in the Blue Ridge (County 723)	
Mike Degree	Old Time Fiddlers' Contest 7/30/77 (Green Mountain 1062)	
Fennig's All-Star String Band	The Hammered Dulcimer (Front Hall 01)	
The Kentucky Colonels	Living in the Past (Briar 4202)	
Clark Kessinger	Live at Union Grove (Folkways FA 2337)	
Bill Monroe	Bluegrass Ramble (MCA-88—formerly Decca DL7-4266)	
New Lost City Ramblers	Vol. 5 (Folkways FA 2395)	
Plank Road String Band	Vocal and Instrumental Blend (June Appal 015)	

Art Rosenbaum	The Art of the Mountain Banjo (Kicking Mule 203)	
Doc Watson	Two Days in November (Poppy PP-LA210-G 0698)	

Old Molly Hare

Haywood Blevins	Old Originals, Vol. II (Rounder 0058)	
Bob Douglas	Old Time Dance Tunes from Sequatchie Valley (Tennvale 001S)	
Clayton McMichen	Old-Time Fiddle Classics, Vol. 2 (County 527)	
*New Lost City Ramblers	Vol. 5 (Folkways FA 2395)	
Art Rosenbaum	The Art of the Mountain Banjo (Kicking Mule 203)	
Roger Sprung	Progressive Bluegrass, Vol. 3 (Folkways FA 2472)	

Old Mother Flanagan

Wilson Douglas	The Right Hand Fork of Rush's Creek (Rounder 0047)	
*Fuzzy Mountain String Band	Same (Rounder 0010)	
Kenny Hall and the Sweets Mill String Band	Same (Bay 727)	

Opera Reel

Arm and Hammer String Band	Stay on the Farm (Fretless 136)	
*Norman Blake	Rising Fawn String Ensemble (Rounder 0122)	
Grant Lamb	Tunes from Home (Voyager 312-S)	

Opus 57

*The David Grisman Quintet	Same (Kaleidoscope F-5)	
Muleskinner	Same (Ridge Runner 0016)	

Over the Waterfall

Norman Blake	Rising Fawn String Ensemble (Rounder 0122)	
John Burke	Fancy Pickin' and Plain Singing (Kicking Mule 202)	
*Fennig's All-Star String Band	The Hammered Dulcimer (Front Hall 01)	

Bill Gareau	Old Time Fiddler's Contest 7/30/77 (Green Mountain 1062)

Ozark Rag

*East Texas Serenaders	1927-1936 (County 410)
Charlie Turner	Ragtime 2 (RBF 18)

Paddy on the Railroad

Ebenezer	Tell It to Me (Biograph 6007)

Paddy on the Turnpike IA

*Graham Townsend	Le Violon/The Fiddle (Rounder 7002)
Joseph Cormier	Scottish Violin Music of Cape Breton (Rounder 7001)

Paddy on the Turnpike IB

Kenny Baker	Farmyard Swing (County 775)
Berline, Bush, and O'Connor	In Concert (Omac-2)
The Dillards with Byron Berline	Pickin' and Fiddlin' (Elektra EKS 7285)
Joe Greene	Joe Greene's Fiddle Album (County 722)
*Bobby Hicks	Texas Crapshooter (County 772)

Appears as **Paddy on the Handcar.**

Thomas Hunter	Deep in Tradition (June Appal 007)

Appears as **Paddy on the Handcar.**

The Red Headed Fiddlers	Old-Time Fiddle Classics, Vol. 2 (County 527)
Roger Sprung	Grassy Licks (Folkways FTS 31036)
Benny and Jerry Thomasson	A Jam Session (Voyager 309)

(Paddy on the Turnpike II)

Wilson Douglas	The Right Hand Fork of Rush's Creek (Rounder 0047)

(Paddy on the Turnpike IIIA)

Clark Kessinger	Volume 2 (County 747)

(Paddy on the Turnpike IIIB)

The Backwoods Band	Jes' Fine (Rounder 0128)

Padraic O'Keefe's Slide

*Boys of the Lough	Second Album (Rounder 3006)

Appears as **Denis Murphy's Slide**

Chieftains	Chieftains 3 (Island ILPS 9379)
How to Change a Flat Tire	A Point of Departure (Front Hall 09)

Pigeon on the Gate

Kevin Burke	Promenade (Mulligan 028)
Jean Carignan	Old Time Fiddle Tunes (Folkways FG 3531)
*Jean Carignan	Plays Coleman, Morrison, and Skinner (Philo 2018)
Frankie Gavin	Traditional Music of Ireland (Shanachie 29008)
Brendan Mulvihill	The Flax in Bloom (Green Linnet 1020)
Tommy Peoples and Paul Brady	The High Part of the Road (Shanachie 29003)
The Riendeau Family	Old-Time Fiddling (County 725)
Eric Thompson	Kicking Mule's Flat Picking Guitar Festival (Kicking Mule 206)

Planxty Drury

*Eugene O'Donnell	Slow Airs and Set Dances (Green Linnet 1015)
Jake Walton and Roger Nicholson	Bygone Days (Front Hall 015)

Planxty George Brabazon

Derek Bell	Carolan's Receipt (Claddagh CC18)
John McCutcheon	The Wind That Shakes the Barley (June Appal 014)
*Yankee Ingenuity	Kitchen Junket (Fretless 200A)

Planxty Irwin

Planxty — Same (Shanachie 79009)

Fennig's All-Star String Band — The Hammered Dulcimer Strikes Again (Front Hall 010)

President Garfield's Hornpipe

Cape Breton Symphony — Fiddle (Glencoe 001)

Jerry Holland — Same (Rounder 7008)

Miller and Miller — Castles in the Air (Philo 119)

Appears as **Blue Water Hornpipe.**

? — 25 Old Tyme Fiddle Hits (K-Tel FH1)

Quince Dillon's High D

Fuzzy Mountain String Band — Summer Oaks and Porch (Rounder 0035)

Ragtime Annie

Kenny Baker — Baker's Dozen (County 730)

Byron Berline — Dad's Favorites (Rounder 0100)

Curly Ray Cline — Chicken Reel (Rebel 1498)

Bob Douglas — Old Time Dance Tunes from Sequatchie Valley (Tennvale 001S)

Fennig's All-Star String Band — The Hammered Dulcimer (Front Hall 01)

John Francis — You Be the Judge (American Heritage 515)

Wilfred Guillette — Old Time Fiddlin' (Green Mountain 1061)

Clark Kessinger — Fiddler (Folkways FA 2336)

Clark Kessinger — The Legend of Clark Kessinger (County 733)

The Kessinger Brothers — Old-Time Fiddle Classics (County 507)

Benny Martin — The Fiddle Collection (CMH 9006)

Bill Northcutt — Fiddle Hoedown (Stoneway 148)

Ted Powers — Old Time Fiddler (Mag 1018)

The Riendeau Family — Old-Time Fiddling (County 725)

Eck Robertson — Master Fiddler (Sonyatone 201)

Buck Ryan — Draggin' the Bow (Rebel 1552)

Roger Sprung — Progressive Bluegrass, Vol. 3 (Folkways FA 2472)

? — 25 Old Tyme Fiddle Hits (K-Tel FH1)

Bill Wimberly — Instrumentals Country Style (Mercury SRW 16261)

Yankee Ingenuity — Kitchen Junket (Fretless 200A)

Rawhide

Carl Jackson — Bluegrass Festival (Prize 498-02)

The Kentucky Colonels — 1965-1967 (Rounder 0070)

*Bill Monroe — Bluegrass Instrumentals (Decca DL 74601)

The White Brothers — Live in Sweden (Rounder 0073)

Red Haired Boy

Appears as **The Red Headed Irishman.**

J.P. and Annadeene Fraley — Wild Rose of the Mountain (Rounder 0037)

Appears as **Little Beggerman.**

Kenny Hall and the Sweets Mill String Band — Same (Bay 727)

Appears as **Little Beggerman.**

Doc Watson — Two Days in November (Poppy PP-LA210-G 0698)

Richmond Cotillion

Delaware Water Gap — Fox Hollow String Band Festival (Biograph 6008)

Rickett's Hornpipe

John Ashby — Down on Ashby's Farm (County 745)

Wilfred Guillette — Old Time Fiddlin' (Green Mountain 1061)

Bill Keith — Something Auld, Something Newgrass, Something Borrowed, Something Bluegrass

Clark Kessinger — Old-Time Music (Rounder 0004)

Roger Sprung — Progressive Bluegrass, Vol. 3 (Folkways FA 2472)

Rights of Man

Ken Bloom	Same (Flying Fish 051)
Fennig's All-Star String Band	The Hammered Dulcimer (Front Hall 01)
Dave Swarbrick and Friends	The Ceilidh Album (Sonet 764)

Roanoke

Kenny Baker and Bobby Hicks	Darkness on the Delta (County 782)
*Bill Monroe	Greatest Hits (MCA-17—formerly Decca DL7-5010)
Muleskinner	Same (Ridge Runner 0016)

Rock the Cradle Joe

James Leva and Bruce Molsky	An Anthology (Tennvale 004)
The Old Virginia Fiddlers	Rare Recordings (County 201)
*Plank Road String Band	Vocal and Instrumental Blend (June Appal 015)
David Winston	Southern Clawhammer Banjo (Kicking Mule 213)

Rocky Mountain Goat

*John Ashby	Down on Ashby's Farm (County 745)
Mose Coffman	Shaking down the Acorns (Rounder 0018)

Rocky Road to Dublin I

Dave Swarbrick	Swarbrick 2 (Transatlantic 341)

(Rocky Road to Dublin II)

Kenny Baker	Dry and Dusty (County 744)

(Rocky Road to Dublin III)

Wilson Douglas	The Right Hand Fork of Rush's Creek (Rounder 0047)

Rodney's Glory

Old Reliable String Band	Same (Folkways FA 2475)

Rose Division

Hollow Rock String Band	Same (Rounder 0024)

Rose Tree I

Fennig's All-Star String Band	Saturday Night in the Provinces (Front Hall 05)

(Rose Tree II)

Kenny Hall	Same (Philo 1008)

Route, The

Hollow Rock String Band	Same (Rounder 0024)

Run, Johnny, Run A

*Kenny Baker	Grassy Fiddle Blues (County 750)

Appears as **Run, Nigger, Run.**

Earl Collins	That's Earl (Briar 0798)
J.P. and Annadeene Fraley	Wild Rose of the Mountain (Rounder 0037)
Tommy Jackson	Square Dances without Calls (MCA-162)

Appears as **Run, Nigger, Run.**

Gid Tanner and the Skillet Lickers	Hear These New Southern Fiddle and Guitar Records (Rounder 1005)

(Run, Johnny, Run B)

Appears as **Run, Boy, Run.**

Eck Robertson	Master Fiddler (Sonyatone 201)

Appears as **Run, Smoke, Run.**

Doc Roberts	Classic Fiddle Tunes (Davis Unlimited 33015)

Rye Straw

The Backwoods Band	Jes' Fine (Rounder 0128)
Bob Carlin	Fiddle Tunes for Clawhammer Banjo (Rounder 0132)
Earl Collins	That's Earl (Briar 0798)
Bob Douglas	Old Time Dance Tunes from Sequatchie Valley (Tennvale 001S)
*Ebenezer	Tell It to Me (Biograph 6007)

Pickin' around the Cookstove	Same (Rounder 0040)	
Doc Roberts	Old-Time Fiddle Classics, Vol. 2 (County 527)	
John Summers	Fine Times at our House (Folkways FS 3809)	
Gid Tanner and the Skillet Lickers	Hear These New Southern Fiddle and Guitar Records (Rounder 1005)	

Sail Away Ladies IA

Susan Cahill	Southern Clawhammer Banjo (Kicking Mule 213)
*Highwoods String Band	No. 3 Special (Rounder 0074)
New Lost City Ramblers	Vol. 5 (Folkways FA 2395)

Sail Away Ladies IB

Kenny Baker	Baker's Dozen (County 730)

(Sail Away Ladies IC)

Otis Burris	Virginia Breakdown (County 705)

Sail Away Ladies II

J.P. and Annadeene Fraley	Wild Rose of the Mountain (Rounder 0037)

(Sail Away Ladies III)

Tommy Jarrell	Sail Away Ladies (County 756)

Sailor's Hornpipe

Bill Monroe	Bluegrass Instrumentals (Decca DL 74601)
Hubert and Ted Powers	Two Generations of Old Time Fiddle (Mag)
Roger Sprung	Progressive Bluegrass Vol. 3 (Folkways FA 2472)

Saint Anne's Reel

Louis Beaudoin	Same (Philo 2000)
Wilfred Guillette	Old Time Fiddlin' (Green Mountain 1061)
Thomas Hunter	Deep in Tradition (June Appal 007)
Theresa and Marie MacLellan	A Trip to Mabou Ridge (Rounder 7006)
John McCutcheon	The Wind That Shakes the Barley (June Appal 014)

Kirsten Nordstrom	Old Time Fiddlers' Contest 7/26/75 (Green Mountain 1050)
The Riendeau Family	Old-Time Fiddling (Country 725)
Henry Sapoznik	Melodic Clawhammer Banjo (Kicking Mule 209)
?	25 Old Tyme Fiddle HIts (K-Tel FH1)
Vivian Williams and Barbaara Lamb	Twin Sisters (Voyager 316-S)

(Sally Ann A)

*John Ashby	Old Virginia Fiddling (County 727)
Clell Caudill	Old Originals, Vol. II (Rounder 0058)
Cockerham, Jarrell, and Jenkins	Back Home in the Blue Ridge (County 723)
Delaware Water Gap	From the Rivers of Baby-lon to the Land of Jazz (Kicking Mule 205)
Pat Dunford	The Old-Time Banjo in America (Kicking Mule 204)
The Hill-Billies	Same (County 405)
Hollow Rock String Band	Same (Rounder 0024)

Sally Ann B

*Fuzzy Mountain String Band	Same (Rounder 0010)
Tommy Jarrell	Come and Go with Me (County 748)

(Sally Ann C)

John Burke	Fancy Pickin' and Plain Singing (Kicking Mule 202)
Doc Roberts	Classic Fiddle Tunes (Davis Unlimited 33015)

Sally Goodin'

Kenny Baker	Dry and Dusty (County 744)
Berline, Bush, and O'Connor	In Concert (Omac-2)
Country Gazette	Live (Antilles 7014)
Dan Crary	Lady's Fancy (Rounder 0099)
J.D. Crowe and the New South	Same (Rounder 0044)

Dave Ferguson and Friends	Somewhere over the Rainbow (Ridge Runner 0003)
J.C. Gentle and Bill Mitchell	Fiddle Jam Session (Voyager 301)
Jana Grief	I Love Fiddlin' (American Heritage 516)
John Hickman	Don't Mean Maybe (Rounder 0101)
Clark Kessinger	Fiddler (Folkways FA 2336)
Clark Kessinger	The Legend of Clark Kessinger (County 733)
Clark Kessinger	Live at Union Grove (Folkways FA 2337)
Bill Long and Bill Mitchell	More Fiddle Jam Sessions (Voyager 304)
Sonny Miller	Virginia Breakdown (County 705)
New Lost City Ramblers	Vol. 2 (Folkways FA 2397)
Poor Richard's Almanac	Same (American Heritage 25)
Bartow Riley	Texas Hoedown (County 703)
Butch Robbins	Forty Years Late (Rounder 0086)
Eck Robertson	Master Fiddler (Sonyatone 201)
Art Rosembaum	Five String Banjo (Kicking Mule 208)
Ace Sewell	Southwest Fiddlin' (Voyager 319-S)
Scotty Stoneman	Live in L.A. (Briar 4201)
Marion Sumner	Road to Home (June Appal 030)
Thomasson, Shorty, Morris, and O'Connor	A Texas Jam Session (Omac-1)
?	25 Old Tyme Fiddle Hits (K-Tel FH1)
Paul Warren	America's Greatest Breakdown Fiddle Player (CMH 6237)
The White Brothers	Live in Sweden (Rounder 0073)
Johnnie Lee Wills	Tulsa Swing (Rounder 1027)
Winnie Winston	Steel Wool (Philo 1058)

Sally in the Garden

*John McCutcheon	The Wind That Shakes the Barley (June Appal 014)
Pickin' around the Cookstove	Same (Rounder 0040)

Sally Johnson

Dick Barrett	You Be the Judge (American Heritage 515)
Byron Berline	Fiddle Jam Session (Voyager 301)
The Dilliards with Byron Berline	Pickin' and Fiddlin' (Elektra EKS 7285)
Jana Greif	I Love Fiddlin' (American Heritage 516)
Herman Johnson	Champion Fiddlin' (American Heritage 1)
Appears as **Sally Ann Johnson.**	
Clark Kessinger	Fiddler (Folkways FA 2336)
Appears as **Sally Ann Johnson.**	
Clark Kessinger	The Legend of Clark Kessinger (County 733)
Fiddlin' Van Kidwell	Same (Vetco 502)
The Lewis Brothers	Texas Farewell (County 517)
Bill Long	Fiddle Fam Session (Voyager 301)
Michael and McCreesh	Dance, Like a Wave of the Sea (Front Hall 017)
Mark O'Connor	National Junior Fiddle Champion (Rounder 0046)
*Eck Robertson	Master Fiddler (Sonyatone 201)
Ace Sewell	Southwest Fiddlin' (Voyager 319-S)
Ervin Solomon, Jim Solomon, and Joe Hughes	Texas Farewell (County 517)
Vernon Solomon	Texas Hoedown (County 703)
Lowe Stokes	Georgia Fiddle Bands Vol. 2 (County 544)
Benny and Jerry Thomasson	A Jam Session (Voyager 309)

Thomasson, Shorty, Morris, and O'Connor	A Texas Jam Session (Omac-1)
Paul Warren	America's Greatest Breakdown Fiddle Player (CMH 6237)
Vivian Williams and Barbara Lamb	Twin Sisters (Voyager 316-S)

Salt River I

Norman Blake	Whiskey Before Breakfast (Rounder 0063)

Appears as **Salt Creek.**

Bottle Hill	Light Our Way along the Highway (Biograph 6009)
Lewis Franklin	Texas Fiddle Favorites (County 707)
Joe Greene	Joe Greene's Fiddle Album (County 722)
John Hickman	Don't Mean Maybe (Rounder 0101)
Clark Kessinger	Old-Time Fiddle Classics Vol. 2 (County 527)
Clark Kessinger	Fiddler (Folkways FA 2336)
Clark Kessinger	The Legend of Clark Kessinger (County 733)

Appears as **Salt Creek.**

Michael and McCreesh	Dance, Like a Wave of the Sea (Front Hall 017)
Benny and Jerry Thomasson	A Jam Session (Voyager 309)

Appears as **Salt Creek.**

Tony Trischka	Banjoland (Rounder 0087)
Doc Watson	On Stage (Vanguard VSD 9/10)

(Salt River II)

Sam Connor	Old Originals—Vol. 1 (Rounder 0057)

Sandy River Belle A

*Fennig's All-Star String Band	The Hammered Dulcimer (Front Hall 01)
Clark Kessinger	The Legend of Clark Kessinger (County 733)
Clark Kessinger	Fiddler (Folkways FA 2336)

Buddy Pendleton	Virginia Breakdown (County 705)
Doc Williams	Old Originals—Vol. 1 (Rounder 0057)

(Sandy River Belle B)

Hollow Rock String Band	Same (Rounder 0024)

Santa Anna's Retreat

Norman Blake	Directions (Takoma D-1064)
*Fuzzy Mountain String Band	Summer Oaks and Porch (Rounder 0035)

Say Old Man Can You Play the Fiddle

Appears as **Lady's Fancy.**

Dan Crary	Lady's Fancy (Rounder 0099)
Thomas Hunter	Deep in Tradition (June Appal 007)
Mark O'Connor	National Junior Fiddle Champion (Rounder 0046)

Appears as **Lady's Fancy.**

Poor Richard's Almanac	Same (American Heritage)
Buddy Spicher	Me and My Heroes (Flying Fish 065)

Appears as **Lady's Fancy.**

Benny Thomasson	Texas Hoedown (County 703)
*Jay Ungar and Lyn Hardy	Songs, Ballads, and Fiddle Tunes (Philo 1023)

Scalloway Lasses, Da

Boys of the Lough	Second Album (Rounder 3006)

Sheebeg and Sheemore

Appears as **Sidh Beag Agus Sidh Mor.**

Derek Bell	Carolan's Receipt (Claddagh CC18)
Boys of the Lough	Same (Trailer 2086)
Tom Gilfellon	Kicking Mule's Flat Picking Guitar Festival (Kicking Mule 206)

Appears as **Sí Bheag, Sí Mhor.**

John McCutcheon	The Wind That Shakes the Barley (June Appal 014)

Appears as **Sí Bheag, Sí Mhor.**

Planxty	Same (Shanachie 79009)
Marie Rhines	The Reconciliation (Fretless 118)
Dave Swarbrick	Swarbrick 2 (Transatlantic 341)

Appears as **Sí Bheag, Sí Mhor.**

Trapezoid	Three Forks of Cheat (Rounder 0113)

Ship in the Clouds

Bob Carlin	Melodic Clawhammer Banjo (Kicking Mule 209)
*Ship in the Clouds	Old Time Instrumental Music (Folkways 31062)

Ships Are Sailing

Gail Mulvihill and Mick Moloney	Irish Music: The Living Tradition Vol. 2 (Green Linnet 1022)
Trapezoid	Three Forks of Cheat (Rounder 0113)

Silver Spire, The

Appears as **Great Eastern Reel.**

Alistair Anderson	Dookin' for Apples (Front Hall 020)

Appears as the second tune of **Pat Sweeney's Medley.**

*Jean Carignan	Same (Philo 2001)

Appears as **La Grondeuse.**

Donna Hinds	Old Time Fiddling 1976 (Fretless 122)

Appears as **John Brennan's Reel.**

Matt Molloy, Paul Brady, and Tommy Peoples	Same (Mulligan 017)

Appears as **John Breenan's Reel.**

Tara Ceili Band	Irish Music: The Living Tradition, Vol. 2 (Green Linnet 1022)

Sleep Soond Ida Moarnin'

*Anderson, Bain, Hunter, and Tulloch	The Silver Bow (Philo 2019)
Boys of the Lough	Same (Trailer 2086)

Sligo Maid, The

Barry, Gorman, Ennis, and Heaney	Irish Music in London Pubs (Folkways FG 3575)
Kevin Burke	Sweeney's Dream (Folkways FW 8876)
Eire Og Ceili Band	Irish Music: The Living Tradition (Green Linnet 1009)
Sean McGuire	Ireland's Champion Traditional Fiddler (Outlet 1031)

Smith's Reel

Norman Solomon	Texas Fiddle Favorites (County 707)
Sumner and McReynolds	Old Friends (Mag 3901)
*Johnnie Lee Wills	Tulsa Swing (Rounder 1027)

Snoring Mrs. Gobeil

*Jean Carignan	Same (Philo 2001)

Appears as **La Ronfleuse Gobeil.**

Jean Carignan	French Canadian Fiddle Songs (Legacy 120)
Jean Carignan	Old Time Fiddle Tunes (Folkways FG 3531)
Frank Ferrel	Fiddle Tunes (Voyager 320-S)

Appears as **Ronfleuse Gobeil.**

Graham Townsend	Le Violon/The Fiddle (Rounder 7002)

Snowflake Reel

Andy Cahan	Melodic Clawhammer Banjo (Kicking Mule 209)
Delaware Water Gap	String Band Music (Adelphi 2004)
Bobby Hicks	Texas Crapshooter (County 772)
Tommy Jackson	Square Dances without Calls (MCA 162)
Brother Oswald and Charlie Collins	Oz and Charlie (Rounder 0060)
?	25 Old Tyme Fiddle Hits (K-Tel FH1)

Snow Shoes A

Ace Sewell	Southwest Fiddlin' (Voyager 319-S)
*Blaine Sprouse	Same (Rounder 0117)

(Snow Shoes B)

John Ashby	Fiddling by the Hearth (County 773)

Soldier's Joy

Anderson, Bain, Hunter, and Tulloch	The Silver Bow (Philo 2019)
Michael Aumen	Kicking Mule's Flat Picking Guitar Festival (Kicking Mule 206)
Jay Belt	Fiddlin' Jay Belt (American Heritage 510)
Curly Ray Cline	Chicken Reel (Rebel 1498)

Appears as first tune of **Soldier's Joy Medley.**

The Hill-Billies	Same (County 405)
Thomas Hunter	Deep in Tradition (June Appal 007)
Tommy Jarrell	Sail Away Ladies (County 756)
The Kentucky Colonels	1965-1967 (Rounder 0070)
Muleskinner	Same (Ridge Runner 0016)
New Lost City Ramblers	Remembrance of Things to Come (Folkways FTS 31035)
New Lost City Ramblers	String Band Instrumentals (Folkways FA 2492)
Hubert and Ted Powers	Powers Town Music (Mag)
Art Rosenbaum	The Art of the Mountain Banjo (Kicking Mule 203)
The Skillet Lickers	Old Time Tunes (County 506)
Gid Tanner's Skillet Lickers	Hell Broke Loose in Georgia (County 514)
Tony Trischka	Heartlands (Rounder 0062)
?	25 Old Tyme Fiddle Hits (K-Tel FH1)
Loyd Wanzer	Plain and Fancy Fiddlin' (American Heritage 19A)
Doc Watson	At Folk City (Folkways FA 2426)
The White Brothers	Live in Sweden (Rounder 0073)
Various Artists	Will the Circle Be Unbroken (United Artists 9801)

Sonny's Mazurka

Boys of the Lough	Live (Philo 1026)
Chieftains	Chieftains 3 (Island ILPS 9379)
*Delaware Water Gap	From the Rivers of Babylon to the Land of Jazz (Kicking Mule 205)

Southwind

Appears as An **Ghaoth Aneas.**

*Chieftains	Chieftains (Island ILPS 9379)
Jerry Jenkins	Fox Hollow String Band Festival (Biograph 6008)
Michael and McCreesh	Dance, Like a Wave of the Sea (Front Hall 017)

Speed the Plow

Arm and Hammer String Band	Stay on the Farm (Fretless 136)
Frank Ferrel	Fiddle Tunes (Voyager 320-S)
Matt Molloy, Paul Brady, and Tommy Peoples	Same (Mulligan 017)
Henry Sapoznik	Melodic Clawhammer Banjo (Kicking Mule 209)
Joe Shannon and Johnny McGreevy	The Noonday Feast (Green Linnet 1023)
J. Scott Skinner	The Strathspey King (Topic 12T280)

Star above the Garter, The

Chieftains	Chieftains 4 (Claddagh CC14)

Star of Munster, The

Kevin Burke	If the Cap Fits (Mulligan 021)
Kathleen Collins	Same (Shanachie 29002)
Seamus Creagh	An Fhidil Straith II (Gael-Linn 069)
Fennig's All-Star String Band	Saturday Night in the Provinces (Front Hall 05)
Frankie Gavin	Traditional Music of Ireland (Shanachie 29008)
The Irish Tradition	The Corner House (Green Linnet 1016)

Maurice Lennon	An Fhidil Straith (Gael-Linn 068)
Martin Mulvihill	Traditional Irish Fiddling from County Limerick (Green Linnet 1012)

Star of the County Down

*Fennig's All-Star String Band	Saturday Night in the Provinces (Front Hall 05)
Michael and McCreesh	Dance, Like a Wave of the Sea (Front Hall 017)
Ned Phoenix	Old Time Fiddlers' Contest 7/30/77 (Green Mountain 1062)
Yankee Ingenuity	Kitchen Junket (Fretless 200A)

Staten Island

Fennig's All-Star String Band	Saturday Night in the Provinces (Front Hall 05)
Grass Food and Lodging	High Class Bluegrass (Ramblin' 02)
John McCutcheon	The Wind That Shakes the Barley (June Appal 014)
Henry Sapoznik	Melodic Clawhammer Banjo (Kicking Mule 209)

Stone's Rag

Byron Berline	Dad's Favorites (Rounder 0100)
*New Lost City Ramblers	String Band Instrumentals (Folkways FA 2492)
Chubby Wise	Chubby Wise and His Fiddle (Stoneway 104)

Stoney Creek

Kenny Baker and Joe Greene	High Country (County 714)
Carl Jackson	Bluegrass Festival (Prize 498-02)
Hubert and Ted Powers	Two Generations of Old Time Fiddle (Mag)
Tony Rice	Same (Rounder 0085)

Stoney Point

Appears as **Wild Horses.**

Curly Ray Cline	Why Me Ralph? (Rebel 1545)
Lyman Enloe	Fiddle Tunes I Recall (County 762)
Kenny Hall and the Sweets Mill String Band	Same (Bay 727)

Appears as **Wild Horses.**

Clark Kessinger	Old-Time Music (Rounder 0004)
Brother Oswald and Charlie Collins	Oz and Charlie (Rounder 0060)
Red Clay Ramblers	Galax 73 (Tennvale 002)
Tony Rice	Manzanita (Rounder 0092)
Art Rosenbaum	The Art of the Mountain Banjo (Kicking Mule 203)
Oscar and Eugene Wright	Old Time Fiddle (Rounder 0089)

Sugarfoot Rag

Ernie Hunter	All about Fiddling (Stoneway 143)
*Bill Keith	Something Auld, Something Newgrass, Something Borrowed, Something Bluegrass (Rounder 0084)
Buck White	That Down Home Feeling (Ridge Runner 0006)

Sugar Hill

The Bogtrotters	The Original Bogtrotters (Biograph 6003)
*Fuzzy Mountain String Band	Summer Oaks and Porch (Rounder 0035)

Sugar in the Gourd

John Ashby	Down on Ashby's Farm (County 745)
Kahle Brewer	Old-Time Fiddle Classics (County 507)
Fiddlin' John Carson	Old Hen Cackled (Rounder 1003)
Earl Collins	That's Earl (Briar 0798)
Fred Sokolow	Bluegrass Banjo Inventions (Kicking Mule 212)
Gid Tanner and the Skillet Lickers	Hear These New Southern Fiddle and Guitar Records (Rounder 1005)
Vivian Williams and Barbara Lamb	Twin Sisters (Voyager 316-S)

Swallow's Tail Reel, The

Barry, Gorman, Ennis, and Heaney	Irish Music in London Pubs (Folkways FG 3575)
Michael Coleman	The Legacy of Michael Coleman (Shanachie 33002)

Dave Swarbrick and Friends	The Ceilidh Album (Sonet 764)

Swallow Tail Jig, The

Fennig's All-Star String Band	Saturday Night in the Provinces (Front Hall 05)
Dave Swarbrick	Swarbrick 2 (Transatlantic 341)

Swinging on a Gate

Father Charles Coen	Farther Charlie (Green Linnet 1021)
*Delaware Water Gap	From the Rivers of Baby-lon to the Land of Jazz (Kicking Mule 205)
Eire Og Ceili Band	Irish Music: The Living Tradition (Green Linnet 1009)
Fennig's All-Star String Band	Saturday Night in the Provinces (Front Hall 05)
Tom Gilfellon	Kicking Mule's Flat Picking Guitar Festival (Kicking Mule 206)
Dudley Laufman	Swinging on a Gate (Front Hall 03)

Take Me back to Georgia

Appears as **Boston Boy.**

David Grisman	Rounder Album (Rounder 0069)

Appears as **Katy Did.**

Sonny Miller	Virginia Breakdown (County 705)
*New Lost City Ramblers	String Band Instrumentals (Folkways FA 2492)
Pickin' around the Cookstove	Same (Rounder 0040)

Tarbolton Reel

Arm and Hammer String Band	New England Contra Dance Music (Kicking Mule 216)

Appears as the first tune of the **Tarbolton Reel Medley.**

*Jean Carignan	Same (Philo 2001)
Michael Coleman	The Wheels of the World (Shanachie 33001)

Appears as **Tarbolton Lodge.**

Frank Ferrel	Fiddle Tunes (Voyager 320-S)

Matt Molloy	Same (Mulligan 004)
Graham Townsend	Le Violon/The Fiddle (Rounder 7002)

Temperance Reel

Bottle Hill	Light Our Way along the Highway (Biograph 6009)
Dave Burgot	Fox Hollow String Band Festival (Biograph 6008)

Appears as **The Teetotaller.**

David Curry	My Ireland (Capitol T10028)
Fennig's All-Star String Band	The Hammered Dulcimer (Front Hall 01)
Jerry Holland	Same (Rounder 7008)
John McCutcheon	The Wind That Shakes the Barley (June Appal 104)
Michael and McCreesh	Dance, Like a Wave of the Sea (Front Hall 017)
Tony Rice	Same (Rounder 0085)
Jerry Robichaud	Maritime Dance Party (Fretless 201)

Appears as **Tee-totaller's Fancy.**

Art Rosenbaum	Five String Banjo (Kicking Mule 508)

Texas Gales

*The Hill-Billies	Same (County 405)
Eric Thompson	Kicking Mule's Flat Picking Guitar Festival (Kicking Mule 206)
Doc Watson	Ballads from Deep Gap (Vanguard VSD 6576)
Watson Family	Same (Folkways FA 2366)
Roland White	I Wasn't Born to Rock 'n' Roll (Ridge Runner 0005)
Wretched Refuse	Same (Beet 7003)

There's a Brown Skin Gal

Junior Daugherty	You Be the Judge (American Heritage 515)
Howdy Forrester	Fiddle Hoedown (Stoneway 148)
Jana Greif	I Love Fiddlin' (American Heritage 516)

Herman Johnson	Champion Fiddling (American Heritage 1)
*Eck Robertson	Master Fiddler (Sonyatone 201)
Ship in the Clouds	Old Time Instrumental Music (Folkways 31062)
Luke Smathers String Band	Mountain Swing (June Appal 024)

Three-in-One Two Step

Arm and Hammer String Band	Stay on the Farm (Fretless 136)
*East Texas Serenaders	1927-1936 (County 410)
*East Texas Serenaders	Texas Farewell (County 517)

Timour the Tartar

Cape Breton Symphony	Fiddle (Glencoe 001)
Marie Rhines	The Reconciliation (Fretless 118)
*Dave Swarbrick	Swarbrick (Transatlantic 337)
J. Scott Skinner	The Strathspey King (Topic 12T280)

Tom and Jerry

John Ashby	Old Virginia Fiddling (County 727)
The Dillards with Byron Berline	Pickin' and Fiddlin' (Elektra EKS 7285)
Lyman Enloe	Fiddle Tunes I Recall (County 762)
Major Franklin	Texas Fiddle Favorites (County 707)
*Herman Johnson	Champion Fiddling (American Heritage 1)
Mark O'Connor	Pickin' in the Wind (Rounder 0068)
Lonnie Peerce	Golden Fiddle Tones (American Heritage 24)
Ace Sewell	Southwest Fiddlin' (Voyager 319-S)
Benny Thomasson	Country Fiddling (County 724)
Thomasson, Morris, and O'Connor	A Texas Jam Session (Omac-2)

Too Young to Marry

Cockerham, Jarrell, and Jenkins	Down to the Cider Mill (County 713)

Appears as **Chinky Pin.**

Clark Kessinger	Fiddler (Folkways FA 2336)

Appears as **Chinky Pin.**

Clark Kessinger	The Legend of Clark Kessinger (County 733)

Appears as **Midnight Serenade.**

The Old Virginia Fiddlers	Rare Recordings (County 201)

Appears as **Fourth of July**

Vivian Williams and Barbara Lamb	Twin Sisters (Voyager 316-S)

Turkey in the Straw

Cap Ayers and Darrell Cockham	Old Originals Vol. I (Rounder 0057)
Curly Ray Cline	Clinch Mountain Boy Jailed (Rebel 1566)
Louis Henderson	Fine Times at Our House (Folkways FA 3809)
Clark Kessinger	Live at Union Grove (Folkways FA 2337)
Grant Lamb	Tunes from Home (Voyager 312-S)
Bill Monroe	Bluegrass Time (MCA-116—formerly Decca DL7-4896)
Ray Osborn	More Fiddle Jam Sessions (Voyager 304)
Eck Robertson	Master Fiddler (Sonyatone 201)
Art Rosenbaum	Five String Banjo (Kicking Mule 208)
*Blaine Sprouse	Same (Rounder 0117)
Roger Sprung	Progressive Bluegrass Vol. 3 (Folkways FA 2472)
?	25 Old Tyme Fiddle Hits (K-Tel FH1)

Twinkle Little Star

*Kenny Baker	Kenny Baker Country (County 736)
Curly Ray Cline	Clinch Mountain Boy Jailed (Rebel 1566)
The Dillards with Byron Berline	Pickin' and Fiddlin' (Elektra EKS 7285)
Glenn Feener	Old Time Fiddling 1976 (Fretless 122)

Richard Greene	Duets (Rounder 0075)	
Benny Martin	Big Daddy of the Fiddle and Bow (CMH 9019)	
Benny and Jerry Thomasson	A Jam Session (Voyager 309)	
Loyd Wanzer	Plain and Fancy Fiddlin' (American Heritage 19A)	
Loyd Wanzer	You Be the Judge (American Heritage 515)	
Paul Warren	America's Greatest Breakdown Fiddle Player (CMH 6237)	

Wagoner

Appears as **Tennessee Wagoner.**

Curly Ray Cline	Clinch Mountain Boy Jailed (Rebel 1566)
*The Dillards with Byron Berline	Pickin' and Fiddlin' (Elektra EKS 7285)
Highwoods String Band	No. 3 Special (Rounder 0074)

Appears as **Tennessee Wagon.**

Fiddlin' Van Kidwell	Midnight Ride (Vetco 506)
Bill Long	More Fiddle Jam Sessions (Voyager 304)

Appears as **Jolly Wagoner.**

Conrad Pelletier	Old Time Fiddlers' Contest 7/27/75 (Green Mountain 1050)
Eck Robertson	Old-Time Fiddle Classics Vol. 2 (County 527)
Eck Robertson	Master Fiddler (Sonyatone 201)
Normon Solomon	Texas Fiddle Favorites (County 707)
Benny and Jerry Thomasson	A Jam Session (Voyager 309)

Appears as **Tennessee Wagoner.**

Paul Warren	America's Greatest Breakdown Fiddle Player (CMH 6237)

Appears as **Tennessee Wagoner.**

Vivian Williams and Barbara Lamb	Twin Sisters (Voyager 316-S)

Wake Up Susan I

Appears as **Wake Susan.**

Ed Haley	Parkersburg Landing (Rounder 1010)
John McCutcheon	The Wind That Shakes the Barley (June Appal 014)
Burt Porter	Old Time Fiddlers' Contest 7/30/77 (Green Mountain 1062)
*Red Clay Ramblers	Same (Folkways FTS 31039)
Buck Ryan	Draggin' the Bow (Rebel 1552)

(Wake Up Susan II)

Lyman Enloe	Fiddle Tunes I Recall (County 762)

Walking in My Sleep

*Kenny Baker	Portrait of a Bluegrass Fiddler (County 719)
Curly Ray Cline	Chicken Reel (Rebel 1498)
Kyle Creed	Blue Ridge Style Square Dance Time (Mountain 301)
The Old Virginia Fiddlers	Rare Recordings (County 201)

Western Country

The Bogtrotters	The Original Bogtrotters (Biograph 6003)

Appears as **Suzanna Gal.**

Cockerham, Jarrell, and Jenkins	Down to the Cider Mill (County 713)
*Kyle Creed	Blue Ridge Style Square Dance Time (Mountain 301)

Appears as **Fly Around.**

New Lost City Ramblers	Vol. 3 (Folkways FA 2398)

Appears as **Fly Around.**

Old Reliable String Band	Same (Folkways FA 2375)

Appears as **Susanna Gal.**

The Old Virginia Fiddlers	Rare Recordings (County 201)
Pete Parish	Clawhammer Banjo (Tennvale 003)

Appears as **Fly Around My Pretty Little Miss.**

Ola Belle Reed	Same (Rounder 0021)

West Fork Gals

Wilson Douglas	The Right Hand Fork of Rush's Creek (Rounder 0047)
*Fuzzy Mountain String Band	Summer Oaks and Porch (Rounder 0035)
Hollow Rock String Band	Same (Rounder 0024)
Miller and Miller	Castles in the Air (Fretless 119)
Roaring Ramblers	Galax 73 (Tennvale 002)

Wheel Hoss

Kenny Baker	Kenny Baker Plays Bill Monroe (County 761)
Jerry Douglas	Fluxology (Rounder 0093)
Grass Food and Lodging	High Class Bluegrass (Ramblin' 02)
*Bill Monroe	Bluegrass Instrumentals (Decca DL 74601)

Wheels of the World, The

Kevin Burke	If the Cap Fits (Mulligan 021)
*Seán Keane	Gusty's Frolics (Claddagh CC17)
*James Morrison	The Wheels of the World (Shanachie 33001)
Tommy Peoples and Paul Brady	The High Part of the Road (Shanachie 29003)

Whiskey before Breakfast

Dick Barrett	More Fiddle Jam Sessions (Voyager 304)
Norman Blake	Whiskey before Breakfast (Rounder 0063)
Loyd Wanzer	Plain and Fancy Fiddlin' (American Heritage 19A)

White Cockade, The

Roger Sprung	Grassy Licks (Folkways FTS 31036)
Dave Swarbrick	Swarbrick (Transatlantic 337)
The Scottish Fiddle Festival Orchestra	Scottish Traditional Fiddle Music (Olympic 6151)

White Horse Breakdown

Kenny Baker	Kenny Baker Country (County 736)
Norman Blake	Directions (Takoma D-1064)
*Blaine Sprouse	Same (Rounder 0117)

Wind That Shakes the Barley, The

Mary Bergin	Traditional Irish Music (Shanachie 79006)
John McCutcheon	The Wind That Shakes the Barley (June Appal 014)
Planxty	Cold Blow and the Rainy Night (Shanachie 79011)
Jake Walton and Roger Nicholson	Bygone Days (Front Hall 015)

Wise Maid, The

Garrai Eoin II Ceili	Irish Music: The Living Tradition Vol. 2 (Green Linnet 1022)

Appears following the song **Jolly Beggar.**

Planxty	Same (Shanachie 79009)

Appears following the song **Jolly Beggar.**

Planxty	Planxty Collection (Polydor 2383 397)

A Select Discography

The musician who is not acquainted with the many styles and traditions represented in this book may find the following list useful. I have selected a small number of recordings to outline the breadth of styles in the British Isles and North America. It should be obvious given a list of this size that it is hardly meant to be exhaustive of the stylistic range within a particular genre. It is more in the nature of a sketch; blocking out the whole, showing the scope, rather than rendering the details.

New England

Fennig's All-Star String Band
The Hammered Dulcimer
Front Hall 01

Old-Time

Clark Kessinger, Earl Johnson,
Eck Robertson, Lowe Stokes,
Clayton McMichen, Arthur Smith, and others.
Old-Time Fiddle Classics
County 507

Tommy Jarrell
Sail Away Ladies
County 756

Highwoods String Band
Dance All Night
Rounder 0045

Bluegrass

Bill Monroe
Bill Monroe's Country Music Hall of Fame
MCA 140

Kenny Baker
Frost on the Pumpkin
County 770

Vassar Clements, David Grisman,
Jerry Garcia, Peter Rowan, and John Kahn
Old and in the Way
Round RX103

Texas

Benny Thomasson, Mark O'Connor,
Texas Shorty, and Terry Morris
A Texas Jam Session
Omac-1

Western Swing

Milton Brown and His Brownies, Bill Boyd,
Cliff Bruner's Texas Wanderers, and others.
Beer Parlor Jive
String 801

English

William Kimber
The Art of William Kimber
Topic 12T249

Scottish

J. Scott Skinner
The Strathspey King
Topic 12T280

Shetland

Tom Anderson, Aly Bain,
Trevor Hunter, and Davie Tulloch
The Silver Bow
Philo 2019

Irish

Patrick J. Touhey, Michael Coleman
James Morrison, Tom Ennis, and others.
The Wheels of the World
Shanachie 33001

Kevin Burke, Séamus Creach,
Séan Keane, and Paddy Glackin
An Fhidil Sraith II
Gael-Linn CEF 069

British Isles, general

The Boys of the Lough
Second Album
Rounder 3006

Canada

Jean Carignan
Jean Carignan
Philo 2001

Nova Scotia/Cape Breton

Jerry Holland
Jerry Holland
Rounder 7008

The following artists and recordings will be of great interest to the mandolinist although they do not directly pertain to the playing of fiddle tunes.

Dave Apollon
Mandolin Virtuoso
Yazoo 1066

Jethro Burns
Jethro Burns and *Jethro Live*
Flying Fish 042 and 072

David Grisman Quintet
David Grisman Quintet
Kaleidoscope F-5

Tiny Moore and Jethro Burns
Back to Back
Kaleidoscope F-9

Tiny Moore
Tiny Moore
Kaleidoscope F-12

Andy Statman
Flatbush Waltz
Rounder 0116

Jesse McReynolds (of Jim and Jesse)
The Jim and Jesse Story
CMH 9022

Bill Monroe
Bill Monroe's Country Music Hall of Fame
MCA 140

A Listing of Record Companies

Many of the albums listed in the discography are specialty items and can be difficult to track down even in major record stores. You may find it easier, and less expensive, to order them direct from their manufacturers. Most of those listed below will send a descriptive catalog upon request.

Adelphi Records
P.O. Box 288
Silver Spring , MD 20907

American Heritage Records
1208 Everett
Caldwell, ID 83605

Arhoolie Records
10341 San Pablo Ave.
El Cerrito, CA 94530

Biograph Records
P.O. Box 109
Canaan, NY 12029

Breakwater Records
Box 52
Site C
Portugal Cove, Newfoundland AOA3KO
Canada

Briar Records
11312 Santa Monica Blvd., Suite # 7
Los Angeles, CA 90025

Country Dance and Song Society
505 8th Avenue
New York, NY 10018

CMH Records
P.O. Box 39439
Los Angeles, CA 90039

County Records
P.O. Box 191
Floyd, VA 24091

Folkways Records
43 W. 61st Street
New York, NY 10023

Fretless Records
The Barn
North Ferrisburg, VT 05473

Front Hall Records
R.D. 1, Wormer Road
Voorheesville, NY 12186

Gael Linn Records
26 Cearnog Mhuireean
Baile Atha Cliath 2
Ireland

GMI Records
P.O. Box 401
Marham, Ontario L3P358
Canada

Green Linnet Records
70 Turne Hill Rd.
New Canaan, CT 06840

Green Mountain Records
Garvey Hill
Northfield, VT 05663

June Appal Records
Box 743
Whitesburg, KY 41858

Kicking Mule Records
Box 3233
Berkeley, CA 94703

MAG Records
U.P.S. Inc.
P.O. Box 655
Coeburn, VA 24230

Mulligan Records
The Mews
101 Templeogue Rd.
Dublin 6
Ireland

Omac Records
23207 52nd Ave. West
Mount Lake Terrace, WA 98043

Outlet Records
63-67 Smithfield
Belfast BT11JD
North Ireland

Philo Records
The Barn
North Ferrisburg, VT 05473

Rebel Records
P.O. Box 191
Floyd, VA 24091

Ridge Runner Records
c/o Richey Records
7121 W. Vickery No. 118
Fort Worth, TX 76116

Rounder Records
186 Willow Ave.
Somerville, MA 02144

Shanachie Records
Dalebrook Park
Ho-Ho-Kus, NJ 07423

Sonet Records
121 Ledbury Rd.
London W112AQ
England

United Artists Records
729 Seventh Ave.
New York, NY 10019

Vetco Records
5825 Vine Street
Cincinnati, OH 45216

Voyager Records
424 — 35th Avenue
Seattle, WA 98122

In addition, the avid vinyl fiend should be apprised of the existence of these mail-order record outlets.

They will send their extensive catalogs upon request.

County Sales	Roundup Records
Box 191	Box 147
Floyd, VA 24091	East Cambridge, MA 02141

BIBLIOGRAPHY

Breathnach, Brendán. *Ceol Rince na hÉireann, Cuid 1* (Dublin: Oifig an tSolàthair, 1963).

Breathnach, Brendán. *Ceol Rince na hÉireann, Cuid 2* (Dublin: Oifig an tSolàthair, 1976).

Brody, David. *Kenny Baker/Fiddle* (New York: Oak Publications, 1979).

Bulmer, D. and N. Sharpley. *Music from Ireland, Volume 1*

Christeson, R.P. *The Old-Time Fiddler's Repertory* (Columbia, Missouri: University of Missouri Press, 1973).

Cole, M.M. *One Thousand Fiddle Tunes* (Chicago: M.M. Cole Publishing Co., 1940).

Glaser, Matt. *Teach Yourself Bluegrass Fiddle* (New York: Oak Publications, 1978).

––––––. *Vassar Clements/Fiddle* (New York: Oak Publications, 1978).

Huntington, Gale. *William Litten's Fiddle Tunes* (Massachusetts: Hines Point Publishers,1977).

Kaufman, Alan. *Beginning Old-Time Fiddle* (New York: Oak Publications, 1977)

Karpeles, Maud and Kenworthy Schofield. *101 English Folk Dance Airs* (New York: Hargail Music Press).

Kennedy, Peter. *The Fiddler's Tune-Book* (New York: Hargail Music Press).

––––––. *The Second Fiddler's Tune-Book* (New York: Hargail Music Press).

Krassen, Miles. *Appalachian Fiddle* (New York: Oak Publications, 1973).

Lowinger, Gene. *Bluegrass Fiddle* (New York: Oak Publications, 1974).

Marriot, Beryl and Roger. *Tunes for the Band* (London: The English Folk Dance and Song Society, 1976).

McDermott, Hugh. *Allan's Irish Fiddler* (Glasgow: Mozart Allan).

O'Neill, Francis. *O'Neill's Music of Ireland* (New York: Daniel Michael Collins, 1979).

O'Sullivan, Donal. *Carolan: The Life and Times of an Irish Harper* (London: Routledge and Kegan Paul Limited, 1958).

Phillips, Stacy and Kenny Kosek. *Bluegrass Fiddle Styles* (New York: Oak Publications, 1978).

Perron, Jack and Randy Miller. *Irish Traditional Fiddle Music* (New Hampshire: Fiddle Case Books, 1974).

Richardson, Dave, Aly Bain, Cathal McConnell, and Robin Morton. *Music and Song from the Boys of Lough* (Edinburgh: Gilderoy Music, 1977).

Skinner, J. Scott. *The Scottish Violinist* (Glasgow: Bayley and Ferguson, LTD.).

Sloanaker, Jack and Tony Parkes. *Square Dance Chord Book and Tune Locator* (Vermont: F&W Records, 1979).

Timpany, John. *"And out of his knapsack he drew a fine fiddle"* (London: The English Folk Dance and Song Society, 1973).

Welling, William B. *Welling's Hartford Tunebook* (Hartford: William B. Welling, 1976)

Williamson, Robin. *English, Welsh, Scottish, and Irish Fiddle Tunes* (New York: Oak Publications, 1976).

INDEX OF ALTERNATE TITLES

When two different tunes are sometimes referred to by the same name, I have used "See also" to direct you to the other title which may represent the tune you are looking for (e.g., see *Sally Johnson* and *Sally Ann Johnson*).

All other terms used in the index are self-explanatory.

Apex Reel. See *Gaspé Reel*

Bastraine, La. See *Bastringue, La*
Bastringue, La. Also known as *La Bastraine*
Battle of Aughrim, The. See also *After the Battle of Aughrim*
Beaux of Oak Hill. See *Boys of Bluehill, The*
Behind the Haystack. See *Munster Buttermilk, The*
Blue Water Hornpipe. See *President Garfield's Hornpipe*
Bonnie Polka. See *Jenny Lind Polka*
Boston Boy. See *Take Me back to Georgia*
Boys of Bluehill, The. Also known as *Beaux of Oak Hill*
Brighton Camp. See *Girl I Left behind Me, The*
Brown Skin Gal. See *There's a Brown Skin Gal*
Bunch of Keys II. Also known as *Old Bunch of Keys*

Campbell's Farewell to Red Gap. Also known as *Steph's Reel*
Carolan's Concerto. Also known as *Mrs. Poer*
Castle Jig. See *Kesh Jig, The*
Cattle in the Cane. Also known as *Cattle in the Corn*
Cattle in the Corn. See *Cattle in the Cane*
Charming Molly Brannigan. See *Greenfields of America*
Cherokee Shuffle. See also the related tune *Lost Indian I*
Chief O'Neill's Fancy. See *Chief O'Neill's Favorite*
Chief O'Neill's Favorite. Also known as *Chief O'Neill's Fancy*
Chinky Pin. See *Too Young to Marry*
Cold Frosty Morning. See *Frosty Morning*
Coo Coo's Nest. See *Cuckoo's Nest*
Cooley's Reel. Also known as *Joe Cooley's Reel*
Cuckoo's Nest. Also known as *Coo Coo's Nest*

Dance All Night. Also known as *Give the Fiddler a Dram*
Darling Child. See *Too Young to Marry*
Dawn, The. See *Miller's Reel A*
Dennis Murphy's Slide. See *Padraic O'Keefe's Slide*
Did You Ever See the Devil Uncle Joe. See *Miss McLeod's Reel*
Doherty's Reel. See *Wise Maid, The*
Draggin' the Bow. Also known as *Drag That Fiddle*
Drag That Fiddle. See *Draggin' the Bow*
Durham's Bull. Also known as *Durham's Reel*
Durham's Reel. See *Durham's Bull*

Fairy Dance. See also the related tune *Old Molly Hare*
Fiddler a Dram. See *Give the Fiddler a Dram I*
Fly around My Pretty Little Miss. See *Western Country*
Fourth of July. See *Too Young to Marry*
Friar's Breeches. See *Frieze Breeches*
Frieze Breeches. Also known as *Friar's Breeches* and *Frieze Britches*
Frosty Morning. Also known as *Cold Frosty Morning*

Gal I Left behind Me. See *Girl I Left behind Me*
Gallopede. Also known as *Yarmouth Reel*
Garfield's Hornpipe. See *President Garfield's Hornpipe*
Gaspé Reel. Also known as *Apex Reel*
George Brabazon. See *Planxty George Brabazon*
Georgia Shuffle. See *Hamilton County*
Ghaoth a Bhogann an Eorna, An. See *Wind That Shakes the Barley, The*
Ghaoth Aneas, An. See *Southwind*
Girl I Left behind Me, The. Also known as *Brighton Camp* and *The Gal I Left behind Me*
Give the Fiddler a Dram I. Also known as *Fiddler a Dram* ; See also *Dance All Night*
Going around the World. See *Katy Hill*
Going up Cripple Creek. See *Cripple Creek*
Goodbye Liza Jane. Also known as *Liza Jane*
Great Eastern Reel. See *Silver Spire, The*

Greenfields of America. Also known as *Charming Molly Brannigan;*
    See also the related tune *Old Mother Flanagan*
Green Willis. Also known as *Green Willis the Raw Recruit* and *The Raw
    Recruit*
Grandeuse, La. See *Silver Spire, The*
Growling Old Man and Woman, The. Also known as *The Old Man and
    the Old Woman*

Hamilton County. Also known as *Georgia Shuffle*
Heel and Toe Polka. See *Jenny Lind Polka*
Hell among the Yearlings. Also known as *Trouble among the Yearlings*
Hitchhiker Blues. See *Lee Highway Blues*
Hop High Ladies. See *Miss McLeod's Reel*
Hop Light Ladies. See *Miss McLeod's Reel*
Hop Up Ladies. See *Miss McLeod's Reel*

Isle of Skye. See *Planxty George Brabazon*

Jackson's Breakdown. See *Richmond Cotillion*
Jenny Lind Polka. Also known as *Bonnie Polka* and *Heel and Toe Polka*
Joe Cooley's Reel. See *Cooley's Reel*
John Brennan's Reel. See *Silver Spire, The*
Johnny Doherty's Reel. See *Wise Maid, The*
Jolly Wagoner Reel. See *Wagoner*
Judy's Reel. See *Maid behind The Bar, The*

Katy Did. See also *Take Me back to Georgia*
Katy Hill. Also known as *Going around the World*; See also the related
    tune *Sally Johnson*
Kesh Jig, The. Also known as *Castle Jig* and *Kincora Jig*
Kincora Jig. See *Kesh Jig, The*
King's Head, The. See *Soldier's Joy*

Lady's Fancy. See *Say Old Man Can You Play the Fiddle*
Lancer's Quadrille. See *Off She Goes*
Leather Britches. Also known as *Old Leather Britches*; See also the
    related tune *Lord Macdonald's Reel*
Lee Highway Blues. Also known as *Hitchhiker Blues, Lee Highway
    Ramble, Opry Fiddler's Blues,* and *Talkin' Fiddle Blues*
Liberty. Also known as *Reel de Ti-Jean* and *Tipsy Parson*
Little Beggerman, The. See *Red Haired Boy*
Little Rabbit. Also known as *Rabbit Where's Your Mammy*
Lost Indian I. See also the related tune *Cherokee Shuffle*

Maggie Brown's Favorite. Also known as *Planxty Browne* and *Planxty
    Maggie Brown*
Maid behind the Bar, The. Also known as *Judy's Reel*; See also the
    related C part of *Snoring Mrs. Gobeil*
Manchester Hornpipe. See *Rickett's Hornpipe*
Mason's Apron. See also the related tunes *Jack of Diamonds* and *Wake
    Up Susan I*
McCleod's Reel. See *Miss Mcleod's Reel*
Merrily Kissed the Quaker's Wife. See *Merrily Kiss the Quaker*
Merrily Kiss the Quaker. Also known as *Merrily Kissed the Quaker's
    Wife*
Merry Blacksmith. See *Paddy on the Railroad*
Midnight Serenade. See *Too Young to Marry*
Miller's Reel A. Also known as *The Dawn*
Misses McLoud's Reel. See *Miss Mcleod's Reel*
Miss Mcleod's Reel. Also known as *Did You Ever See the Devil Uncle
    Joe, Hop High Ladies, Hop Light Ladies, Hop Up Ladies*
Molly Put the Kettle on I. Also known as *Polly Put the Kettle On*
Morgan Magan. Also known as *Planxty Morgan Magan*
Mrs. MacLeod's Reel. See *Miss Mcleod's Reel*
Mrs. McCloud's Reel. See *Miss Mcleod's Reel*
Mrs. Poer. See *Carolan's Concerto*
Munster Buttermilk, The. Also known as *Behind the Haystack*
My Love is but a Lassie Yet. See *Too Young to Marry*

New Lee Highway Blues. See *Lee Highway Blues*
New Soldier's Joy. See *Soldier's Joy*

O'Carolan's Concerto. See *Carolan's Concerto*
Off She Goes. Also known as *Lancer's Quadrille*
Old Bunch of Keys. See *Bunch of Keys II*
Old French. Also known as *Rambler's Hornpipe*
Old Leather Britches. See *Leather Britches*

Old Man and Old Woman. See *Growling Old Man and Woman, The*
Old Molly Hare. See also the related tune *Fairy Dance*
Old Mother Flanagan. See also the related tune *Greenfields of America*
Opry Fiddler's Blues. See *Lee Highway Blues*

Paddy on the Handcar. See *Paddy on the Turnpike IB*
Paddy on the Railroad. Also known as *Merry Blacksmith*
Paddy on the Turnpike IB. Also known as *Paddy on the Handcar*
Patty on the Turnpike. See *Paddy on the Turnpike I and II*
Padraic O'Keefe's Slide. Also known as *Dennis Murphy's Slide*
Peter Street. See *Timour the Tartar*
Pig Town Fling. See *Stoney Point*
Planxty Browne. See *Maggie Brown's Favorite*
Planxty Erwin. See *Planxty Irwin*
Planxty George Brabazon. Also known as *George Brabazon* and *Isle of
        Skye*
Planxty Maggie Brown. See *Maggie Brown's Favorite*
Planxty Morgan Magan. See *Morgan Magan*
Plaza Polka. See *Richmond Cotillion*
Polly Put the Kettle On. See *Molly Put the Kettle On I*
President Garfield's Hornpipe. Also known as *Blue Water Hornpipe*
        and *Garfield's Hornpipe*

Rabbit Where's Your Mammy. See *Little Rabbit*
Rambler's Hornpipe. See *Old French*
Red Haired Boy. Also known as *The Little Beggerman* and *The Red
        Headed Irishman*
Reel de Ti-Jean. See *Liberty*
Richmond Cotillion. Also known as *Jackson's Breakdown* and *Plaza
        Polka*
Rickett's Hornpipe. Also known as *Manchester Hornpipe*
Rock the Cradle Joe. See also the related A part of *Sally Ann B*
Ronfleuse Gobeil, La. See *Snoring Mrs. Gobeil*
Run, Johnny, Run A. Also known as *Run, Nigger, Run*
Run, Nigger, Run. See *Run, Johnny, Run A*

Sally Ann B. See also the related tune *Rock the Cradle Joe*
Sally Johnson. Also known as *Sally Ann Johnson*; See also the related
        tune *Katy Hill*
Salt Creek. See *Salt River I*
Salt River I. Also known as *Salt Creek*
Sandy River. See *Sandy River Belle A1*
Sandy River Belle A1. Also known as *Sandy River*
Say Old Man Can You Play the Fiddle. Also known as *Lady's Fancy*
Sheebeg and Sheemore. Also known as *Sí Bhegg Sí Mhor* and *Sidh
        Beag Agus Sidh Mor*
Sí Bhegg Sí Mhor. See *Sheebeg and Sheemore*
Sidh Beag Agus Sidh Mor. See *Sheebeg and Sheemore*
Silver Spire, The. Also known as *Great Eastern Reel, La Grondeuse,*
            and *John Brennan's Reel*
Snoring Mrs. Gobeil. Also known as *La Ronfleuse Gobeil*; See also the
        related B part of *Maid behind the Bar, The*
Soldier's Joy. Also known as *The King's Head*
Southwind. Also known as *An Ghaoth Aneas*
Steph's Reel. See *Campbell's Farewell to Red Gap*
Stoney Point. Also known as *Pig Town Fling, Wild Horses,* and *Wild
        Horses at Stoney Point*
Suzanna Gal. See *Western Country*
Sweet Sixteen. See *Too Young to Marry*

Take Me back to Georgia. Also known as *Boston Boy* and *Katy Did*
Talkin' Fiddle Blues. See *Lee Highway Blues*
Tarbolton Lodge. See *Tarbolton Reel*
Tarbolton Reel. Also known as *Tarbolton Lodge*
Teetotaler's Fancy. See *Temperance Reel*
Teetotaler's Reel. See *Temperance Reel*
Tennessee Wagoner. See *Wagoner*
Texas Gales. Also known as *Texas Gals*
Texas Gals. See *Texas Gales*
Texas Wagoner. See *Wagoner*
There's a Brown Skin Gal. Also known as *Brown Skin Gal*
Timour the Tartar. Also known as *Peter Street*
Tipsy Parson. See *Liberty*
Too Young to Marry. Also known as *Chinky Pin, Darling Child, Fourth
        of July, Midnight Serenade, My Love is but a Lassie Yet,* and
        Sweet Sixteen

Trouble among the Yearlings. See *Hell among the Yearlings*
Twinkle Little Star. Also known as *Twinkle Star; Twinkle, Twinkle*;
    and *Twinkle, Twinkle Little Star*

Wagoner. Also known as *Jolly Wagoner Reel, Tennessee Wagoner*, and
    Texas Wagoner
Wake Up Susan I. See also the related tune *Mason's Apron*
Western Country. Also known as *Fly Around My Pretty Little Miss* and
    Sussanna Gal
West Fork Gals. Also known as *Westfort Gals*
Westfort Gals. See *West Fork Gals*
Wild Horses. See *Stoney Point*
Wild Horses at Stoney Point. See *Stoney Point*
Wind That Shakes the Barley, The. Also known as *An Ghaoth a Bhogann*
Wise Maid, The. Also known as *Doherty's Reel* and *Johnny Doherty's*
    Reel

Yarmouth Reel. See *Gallopede*